STEAM RAILWAY
THE GLORIOUS YEARS

THE GLORIOUS YEARS

RECALLING THE BRITISH STEAM YEARS BEFORE 1968

INTRODUCTION BY NIGEL HARRIS, MANAGING EDITOR *STEAM RAILWAY*

EDITED BY JULIAN HOLLAND

BOXTREE

First published in Great Britain in 1996 by Boxtree Limited

Copyright (text) © individual contributors as credited 1996
Copyright (photographs) © individual contributors as credited
Copyright (*Steam Railway* logo) © EMAP Apex Publications Limited

1 2 3 4 5 6 7 8 9 10

Researched, edited and designed by Julian Holland

Printed and Bound in Great Britain by Jarrold Book Printing, Thetford

Boxtree Limited,
Broadwall House,
21 Broadwall,
London SE1 9PL

A CIP catalogue entry for this book is available from the British Library

ISBN 0 7522 1077 7

Front cover photograph Stanier 2-8-0 No. 48442 passes
Buxworth on a cold and crisp 3 February 1968 (*Paul Riley*)

Back cover photograph Immaculately turned-out Jubilee
No. 45584 *North West Frontier* makes a fine sight hauling
the 4.24pm Carlisle to Manchester through Wreay Cutting
in August 1964 (*Peter J. Robinson*)

Title page photograph During the last month of steam
working over Shap, December 1967, the 8.20am Ribble
Sidings-Carlisle was one of the last remaining steam
turns. With today's 25kv electric traction hauling trains
past this setting at Greenholme at speeds approaching
100mph, in both directions, it is difficult to recollect that
scenes like this ever took place. Recorded for ever in
December 1967 on Kodachrome II, 25ASA film, Paul
Riley's art is seen at its brilliant best. He has exercised
great skill in holding steady his Prinz 400mm telephoto
lens. This long lens has heightened the drama of the
backlit exhausts of both train and banking engines,
superbly exposed for maximum effect. (*Paul Riley*)

Contents

Introduction

Steam Railway's monthly 'Glorious Years' feature is now a famous institution in railway magazine publishing – and it has got quite a pedigree too. It first appeared back in 1981 (in *Steam World*, in those days) and the first contributor in April of that year was the legendary W. J. V. ('Bill') Anderson – whose black and white steam photography inspired a generation of lineside photographers. Armed perhaps with a roll of chemist's shop film and a basic camera, new recruits started out brimming with confidence as they set about photographing the railway scene.

However, the anticipation and mounting excitement of dashing to the chemist's shop to collect the processed results usually led to disappointment. We've all been there! With Bill Anderson's cracking shots from Glenfarg, Beattock or perhaps the West Highlands firmly in our minds and hope in our hearts, we were crushed at our fuzzy grey-and-grey shots, with skew-whiff signals and maybe a smoky speck in the distance which just *might* have been a smokebox door!

Ian Krause, whose photographic style is now rather distinctive (influenced on the one hand by Bill Anderson and on the other by Colin Gifford) and whose portfolio appeared in *Steam World*'s October 1981 issue, recalls such experiences with good humour.

'I was absolutely sold on Anderson's pictures,' he says. 'So, off I went to Scotland to take similar pictures. I was desperately disappointed with the results and it took me ages to figure out why I couldn't make Thornton Junction look like he did!'

Some railway photographers, like Bill Anderson and Eric Treacy, were maybe just born – but the rest of us have to work at it. And work very hard indeed. Like any other specialist technique, railway photography is a skill, an art – and it has to be practised, honed and polished through trial and error, experiment and failure. Then, one day, the combination of hard work, careful thought and good luck (a crucial ingredient!) works in your favour to create a pleasing image, then another – and suddenly you're not only enjoying being out and about on the railway, but you're producing pictures you're proud of. From that point the never-ending quest for the Holy Grail of railway photography, the mythical Master Shot begins in earnest. It's a recipe for massive enjoyment, lots of fresh air, plenty of travel and a treasure trove of happy memories and good company along the way. Yes, steam photography is about far more than just the pictures. An interest in railway photography, as well as being a highly rewarding pastime in its own right, was – and remains – a social framework for some very good times, rich experiences, unforgettable memories and friendships which often last a lifetime.

Steam photography has always been a highly subjective business, of course, and one man's photographic meat is most certainly another's pictorial poison. This debate really hotted up in the 1960s after Colin Gifford triggered the 'New Approach' – the highly artistic style of photography in which mood, feel and impressionism play an important part. Nowadays, it's more widely appreciated and pursued, but it's still rather controversial amongst those of a more traditional outlook. Often, the train is an incidental, small part of an overall composition in which the railway's relationship with the landscape, and the role of people in and around the trains, stations, sheds and yards, play a crucial part in the overall scene.

To those who wished to see the cabside numbers, rivets and a neat exhaust hanging over the train, the often shabby surroundings of canals and mill chimneys, or the prominent wet cobbles of a Lancashire side-street were just too much. Feathers flew, voices were raised and pictures (sometimes literally) were torn apart. But, significantly, more people went out taking pictures, and our wealth of historic photographic images grew quickly in extent and diversity. The steam photographers of the past have created a magnificent legacy which we can all still enjoy and marvel at.

The roll of honour of railway photographers is a long and proud one, and whilst some names are better known than others, we owe a debt of gratitude to each and every one. Can you think of a hobby interest which has been better served (or recorded) by its supporters? I can't. Aircraft spotters? Shipping enthusiasts? Old car fans? I may be wrong, but I don't think so. Hobby photographers have created a record of an industry, a way of life and a transport system which is second to none and quite unequalled in other walks of life. To regular readers of railway books and magazines, the availability of good-quality historic photographs is so wide that I fear we may take this magnificent resource for granted.

The volunteer regiments of railway photographers roamed far and wide over main routes and branches, to industrial railways and workshops, goods yards and engine sheds, carriage works and docksides. Wherever the iron horse went, someone, close by, was usually stalking with a camera and notebook. For decades, their best work was featured in magazines and books, but the importance of railway photography very definitely moved up a gear in the late 1970s, after a motorcycle journalist decided that steam railways and steam photographers weren't getting a fair crack of the whip in the rather staid monthly magazines of the day.

Pausing at Tavistock South, Class '4575' 2-6-2T No. 5541 heads the 5.40pm Launceston-Plymouth on May 2 1961. The line from Plymouth to Tavistock opened in 1859, the extension to Launceston following six years later. The original Tavistock station was burnt down in 1887 and rebuilt in the original style. Short workings between Plymouth and Tavistock were usually push-and-pull trains, hauled by Class '64XX' 0-6-0PTs or suitably fitted Class '4575' 2-6-2Ts, but through trains to Launceston were locomotive-hauled. The line closed from December 31 1962, the last trains being due to run two days previously. In fact the last two trains were snowed up in a fierce blizzard and did not reach their destinations until the following afternoon. No. 5541 survived withdrawal in July 1962, being rescued from Woodhams Yard at Barry by the Dean Forest Railway. (R. C. Riley)

Longhope was on the GWR single line connecting the county towns of Gloucester and Hereford. On November 20 1963 Ben Ashworth was at Longhope to photograph the station with Hereford-Gloucester locals arriving and departing and was invited into the signal box. It was a journey back in time – a pot-bellied stove, an ancient rickety armchair with a latticework of cord to prevent the legs shooting sideways on the polished linoleum and an oil lamp hanging from the ceiling. Almost the only modern item was the tin of Castrol seen on the 'kitchen' table. Although it was to close within a year, a surly relief stationmaster took exception to Ben's presence and he was ordered out. Luckily there had been plenty of time to record the box interior and sample the brew in the handleless teapot. (*Ben Ashworth*)

The face of railway publishing in Britain was changed forever by the vision of *Steam Railway*'s founding editor David Wilcock, who in early 1979 had an idea for a new kind of railway magazine. A railway magazine aimed fair and square at steam-minded folk, a monthly treat in words and pictures, and a regular feast of news. In Peterborough, he persuaded the magazine publishing company Emap to take a gamble with the idea and *Steam Railway* was born. For the first time, the professional skills of the trained journalist were fused with the knowledge and interests of a passionately motivated steam enthusiast. David's instincts were proved right: the magazine has been Britain's best-selling railway magazine ever since.

After a short spell away from Emap in the early 1980s, editing *Steam World*, David came back to *Steam Railway* in early 1984, bringing with him 'The Glorious Years' – and it's been a permanent part of the magazine ever since. The feature plays a very important part in the magazine's editorial mix. *Steam Railway*'s prime job is to be the automatic first choice for anyone interested in today's steam scene. 'TGY' provides a fascinating glance over our editorial shoulder, back into the era whose passing gave birth to the preservation movement. 'TGY' keeps our feet on the ground, reminds us where today's steam business came from – and gives us a chance to wallow in first-class nostalgia.

But it's much more than that. As a schoolboy, I remember poring over the pictures by Ivo Peters, Brian Morrison, Dick Riley and all the rest, but I always wondered who they were, what they looked like, what they did for a living and what sort of cameras they used. For the first time, 'The Glorious Years' answered all those questions and as a reader in those days I began to feel that

I knew my photographic heroes a little better. It made those famous names seem more real, more human and, yes, I began to see them as friends, even though I'd never spoken to them.

Since 1981, and at the time of going to press, a grand total of 155 photographers had seen their 'TGY' portfolios in print, and whilst it isn't possible to name them all here (see p.160), I'd like to take this opportunity to acknowledge with heartfelt thanks the trouble they've gone to over the years not just in producing their wonderful collections of images, but also in making them available for us all to share and enjoy through the pages of magazines like *Steam Railway* and *Steam World*. By putting their work into print, those of us who never knew the Somerset & Dorset route, the Highland main line, the 'Withered Arm' and a thousand other pieces of railway, have been given a rare second chance to appreciate their beauty and appeal. For that, I'm sure I speak for thousands of other folk in taking this opportunity just to say 'thanks'.

When Julian Holland came to see me to discuss this project, I was filled with apprehension when he said: 'Can you choose 15 contributors who can give us good material and widespread geographical coverage?' What a question! How on earth were we to make the choice – because each and every 'TGY' we've published over the years has had its own unique strengths, its own special appeal. The contributors whose work you'll enjoy in this book would, I'm sure, quickly and modestly dismiss any notion that theirs were the best pictures published in this long-running series. That really isn't important. This isn't exactly a random selection, but in picking the contributors, what we've tried to do is assemble a representative collection of names and material. Who knows,

Up trains from Plymouth faced the punishing climb of Hemerdon bank, about four miles, mainly at 1-in-42. Heavy express trains required an assistant engine as far as Newton Abbot since there was also Dainton bank to face beyond Totnes. On July 5 1955, with only a seven-carriage load, 'Castle' class 4-6-0 No. 5098 *Clifford Castle* required no assistance and was recorded near the summit with the 7.30am Penzance-Manchester (London Road), which included through coaches to Birkenhead to be detached at Crewe. (*R. C. Riley*)

if the book goes well, maybe there will be further volumes – why not let us know what you think? And perhaps tell us whose work you'd like to see more of!

A great railway photograph, like beauty, exists in the eye of the beholder; so does great railway art. Some prefer the super-detailed canvas whilst others claim that Turner's famous canvas *Rain, Steam and Speed* is the way to go. You could easily rerun the traditional-versus-impressionist photographic debate and I've wondered how the great Impressionist artists would have reacted to the steam scene of the twentieth century, given a time machine and a camera! They would undoubtedly have warmed to Colin Gifford's 'New Approach', pioneered by him in the 1960s – and the recent huge success of Gifford's book *And Gone For Ever...* proves that they wouldn't have been alone in their admiration.

Some of today's better-known exponents of the 'New Approach', like Ian Smith or Joe Rajczonek, will, when asked, give a quick answer as to who first inspired them to pick up a camera. 'Bill Anderson,' often comes the reply, quick as a flash.

Clearly, David Wilcock's choice of Bill Anderson as the very first 'TGY' contributor was an inspired one and Bill's pictures (more of which appear in this book) set a standard which today's contributors to 'The Glorious Years' are still determined to follow. Successive editors have worked hard to ensure that 'TGY' continues to deliver the goods and current editor Peter Kelly is committed to the continuing quality and appeal of this evergreen aspect of *Steam Railway*. If you've got a collection of historic photographs which haven't seen the light of day, why not give Peter a call at Peterborough? 'The Glorious Years' is still a permanent and popular part of *Steam Railway*, every month.

GWR 0-6-0 No. 2204 halts briefly at Edington Burtle on February 15 1964 with a Highbridge to Evercreech Junction stopping train. Edington Burtle, on the Somerset Levels, was once the junction for the Somerset & Dorset Joint Railway line to Bridgwater which closed on December 1 1952. The Highbridge-Evercreech Junction section, along with the rest of the SDJR, was closed on March 7 1966. A Collett 0-6-0, No. 3205, survives in preservation as a representative of this once numerous class introduced by the GWR in 1930. (*Chris Gammell*)

Putting this book together has been both a privilege and a pleasure and its publication, I believe, is a fine testimony to all the contributors who've seen their work published in the magazine over the years.

In closing, I must acknowledge the hard work of Julian Holland and my colleague Mel Holley, both of whom have spared no effort in getting this book into print. It's a delightful and wonderfully nostalgic evocation of a much-loved era. If you enjoy it only half as much as we've enjoyed working on *The Glorious Years*, then you'll have enjoyed it very much indeed!

Nigel Harris

Nigel Harris
Managing Editor, *Steam Railway*
Peterborough, March 1996

One of Les Nixon's earliest memories of the Hope Valley line is the spectacle of a former LMS Garratt hammering up grade towards Edale with a freight bound for Gowhole. Sadly, by the time he came to know the area intimately the Garratts had long since gone, but fortunately Gowhole yard, set in an unlikely rural setting in north-west Derbyshire, survived into the 1970s. In this scene, taken on the very cold and snowy morning of January 11 1968, Class '5' 4-6-0 No. 45316 and Class '8F' 2-8-0 Nos. 48191 and 48532 are watered and turned prior to working return trips. Today, barely a trace of the yard remains although careful observers will just be able to locate the turntable retaining wall in the dense undergrowth. (*Les Nixon*)

Les Nixon

For me the glorious years of British Railways span two quite distinct periods. The first, and undoubtedly the more interesting, was the immediate post-war years through to the mid-1950s. It was a period in which the number of active steam locomotives was around 20,000 and only a relatively few lines had suffered the indignity of closure. It was also a period when I first began to travel independently and, thanks to my consuming interest in railways, my first acquaintance with many parts of the UK. Alas it was also a time of great financial stringency; it was all I could do to raise the cost of the fare to some of these far-flung places, let alone pay for a decent bed for the night.

The young enthusiasts' monthly bible of the time was undoubtedly *Trains Illustrated*, a splendid magazine published by Ian Allan Ltd which, in addition to interesting and informed articles and up-to-date news, also included a superb selection of contemporary photographs. It was probably the pages of *TI* (and the associated *ABC* guides and *Locoshed* books) which, more than any other factor, generated insatiable desires to visit places like Kittybrewster, Neyland, Three Bridges and Melton Constable. To this day I have an almost complete bound set of *TI* and many a pleasant hour is spent flicking through the pages, remembering the everyday events of yesteryear. The quality of many of the pictures impressed me then and continue to do so even today. The standards attained by the then protagonists of the art of railway photography – F. R. Hebron, E. R. Wethersett, M. W. Earley and W. J. V. (Bill) Anderson, to name but a few – were yardsticks against which many latter-day images are judged. Sadly, my own very limited output of that period fell far short of these exacting standards. I used to think that all that was needed to put matters right was some expensive equipment and film rather than the antique Box Brownie and cheap wartime ex-War Department film. Certainly that would have helped, but I have long realised that the most important ingredient of all in successful picture making are the thoughts and actions of the person behind the camera.

In complete contrast, the emphasis of the latter part of my 'glorious years' era, the mid-1960s through to the end of steam, was one of recording on film the fast disappearing contemporary scene.

You may wonder what happened to the missing ten years? I often reflect whether those years, exclusively devoted to study, girl friends, pop music and motorbikes (not necessarily in that order) were actually wisely spent. Maybe I shall get the opportunity to change things a little if ever the time machine is invented. Utopia to me would certainly be a gadget which could be programmed to take you back for, say, a day to a place and date of your choice – assuming I could safely take my 1990s film and camera with me! We can but dream.

Serious railway photography took off in the mid-1960s coincident with the purchase of my first SLR camera. At the time, such cameras, unlike today, were very much a novelty and there were few on the market. The main contenders were the Pentax S1 series and the Varex cameras from the German company Exakta. The latter were the first of the type to be made, dating from the pre-war period. Two Varex IIa bodies were purchased; I recall that one, complete with a standard f2.8 Tessar lens, cost £65. This may seem a modest sum today but allowing for inflation it was equivalent to an outlay of around £750. The attraction of the SLR was of course the option of interchangeable lenses, although it was to be some time before I was able to afford them. Within a couple of years the standard lens was joined by an excellent 35mm Flektogen, an equally good Tessar 135mm telephoto and a rather indifferent 400mm Meyer Telemegor optic. The latter wasn't really all that much good for railway work, although unfortunately I went through a period when I thought it was God's gift to photography and just about everything was taken with it.

Way back in December 1967, with just four days to go before the end of steam on the WCML, I met a young man at Shap Wells enjoying his very first visit to this north-western mecca of railway enthusiasts. It was a frosty, sunny day and even now I recall his truly euphoric mood. 'What a *fantastic* sight and sound and to think this is the *only* time I shall ever experience it!' He was indeed very fortunate; most of my visits were accompanied by gales and horizontal rain. This picture revives happy summer memories of Tebay. Stanier Class '5' 4-6-0 No. 45295 exchanges 'whistle crows' with the Standard Class '4MT' banker of a long freight to signify the start of a combined slog up the grade to Shap summit.

Chinley North Junction was one of the more interesting locations to watch trains pass by, particularly in the days of steam. By the time up trains for Derby reached this point they were well and truly into their uphill slog to the summit at Peak Forest, 969ft above sea level. It was certainly a challenge for locomotives and crew. Many fine pictures have been taken alongside the signal box where the Hope Valley line diverges to the east. This is a rather more unconventional view, taken on February 3 1968, of the junction close to where the lines fork. On the left, Class '8F' 2-8-0 No. 48442, with a Gowhole to Buxton trip freight, rolls to a halt to allow a green-liveried Class '25' diesel, No. D5276, pass on the up fast with a Northwich-Tunstead empty ICI hopper train. The exceptionally clean condition of the '8F' can be judged even from this distance, the work of dedicated enthusiasts the night before.

I well remember one evening early in 1969 when for the first time I had the good fortune to see some of my slides projected using a Leitz Pradovit. Such was the vast improvement of the projected image compared with my old Gnome Classic, I just could not believe that they were my slides I was looking at! I became convinced that Leica cameras would also make a huge difference to the quality of the slides I was producing, and so the piggy bank was raided yet again to buy a second-hand M3, a non-SLR rangefinder camera but with the facility of interchangeable lenses. A camera incidentally which I still have to this day. In terms of durability, quality and convenience it has no equal. If I have to take just one camera on a trip where weight is of prime consideration

Normanton, the south Yorkshire mining town, was a focal point of railway activity for both the LMS and the LNER, indeed they had adjacent shed premises to the north-east of the station. And incidentally, the station, with its buffet and restaurant facilities, fully reflected its important situation with regard to lines radiating to Leeds, York, Wakefield (and hence the Calder Valley and Standedge trans-Pennine routes) and of course to Sheffield. In this scene looking north from the station, with the shed just out of sight to the right, Stanier Class '5' 4-6-0 No. 44951 picks its way through the plethora of lines and semaphore signals with an up freight for Healey Mills yard in June 1966. Sadly, the equivalent picture today would portray just two through lines.

then it is the M3 and a couple of lenses which are packed.

Latterly, the photographic 'arsenal' has been joined by a Nikon F (1972), Pentax 67 (1973/6 and 83) and Nikon FM2 (1991), plus a couple of antique cameras, a Sanderson and an Ensign quarter plate, which are seldom used.

Early colour work using the Voigtlander IIa (the precursor to the Exaktas) and Kodachrome 1 (8 ASA) film was very difficult indeed, the major problem being the very modest f3.5 aperture lens. Nearly all my slides of that period, not surprisingly, were underexposed.

Successful black and white photography using 35mm is an uphill struggle. In order to obtain that exceptional quality, a photographer has to aim for technical perfection in the negative. A speck of dust, a hair, reticulation, etc., are totally unforgiving with the small 35mm negative and will mean at the very least a great deal of remedial work on the final prints. In 1966 I was invited to join the Railway Photographic Society postal portfolio, run throughout its life by founder member Maurice Earley. Here a group of like-minded enthusiast photographers circulated, and constructively commented upon, prints and transparencies. I soon learned that quality monochrome work was so much easier with medium- or large-format films. Soon a Minolta Autocord 2¼in square twin-lens reflex had to find a place in the camera bag. It also meant of course that I had to obtain another enlarger to deal with the bigger negatives.

In some ways, this decision was a double-edged sword since although the technical quality of my pictures improved overnight, I lost the delightful creativity provided by interchangeable lenses. Many years later I was able to have the best of both worlds when medium-format SLR cameras, such as the Pentax 67, came on the market.

Even the most meticulous photographer, though, has lapses of concentration and occasionally accidents. Over the years I have probably suffered most. The day the fixer was added to the developing tank first, a day's unrepeatable photography was ruined because 125ASA film was exposed at 400ASA, and more recently, a colour transparency film was processed as though it were black and white. Two of the more bizarre incidents occurred in 1965, when, after a few days in Scotland photographing the Caledonian Single No. 123 and *Gordon Highlander*, the film was carefully processed (excellent negatives, of course) and then put to wash using water from the *hot* tap instead of the cold. A dash into the bathroom found the emulsion floating on the surface of

A midwinter view of the north-western approach to Gowhole yard. On January 11 1968, one of those days when it is so cold you can hardly find sufficient flexibility in your forefinger to release the shutter, Class '8F' 2-8-0 No. 48197 eases past the typical Midland Railway signalbox at Gowhole Goods Junction with a trip freight from Newton Heath. At this point the up and down fast lines, the main line to Derby and St Pancras, passed the yard on the extreme west, whereas the later Hope Valley lines bisected the yard. The sidings between the two were used to prepare traffic for dispatch to points west. Note the delightful array of what were presumably the mandatory buckets of sand in case of fire. I wonder if any of them were ever used?

Dove Holes tunnel, on the Manchester-Derby Midland main line had the reputation of being one of the wettest on the whole of the LMS system. Certainly the ingress of water provided ample supplies for nearby Chinley, Gowhole and, I gather, parts of nearby Chapel-en-le-Frith. When this picture was taken, depicting Stanier Class '8F' 2-8-0 No. 48191 bursting from the southern portal on December 18 1967, icicles as well as water could well have been a problem. Note the icefall on the cutting wall to the left of the picture. This photograph was the result of much dedicated effort. During the winter months the sun shines on this precise spot for just 40 minutes each day; it needed no less than seven visits to the location before I finally got the picture I hoped for. Fortunately, in those days lineside photographic permits were easily obtained.

the steaming water. To this day I am convinced that some of the best pictures I ever took were on that roll of film! Just six months later another excellent film was processed and this time correctly washed. It was then hung up to dry, only to be found later totally ruined after the cat had used it to sharpen her claws! The cat was darned near crucified.

Attempting to run before I could walk was certainly true of my early forays into railway photography. Armed with the simplest of cameras I tried to replicate the work of the experts with a singular lack of success. Even when I realised that you couldn't freeze the movement of a 60mph express using a shutter speed of 1/100 second, it still took me a long time to judge to perfection the correct moment to release the shutter. Even so, it hadn't yet occurred to me that telegraph poles sprouting from chimneys, bushes partially obscuring wheels and so on were certainly not *de rigeur*.

Following failure after failure, I was forced to the conclusion that it was

Grindleford is perhaps one of the most scenically located stations in the north of England. Even today the station area boasts a fan of sidings, although the MR goods shed and most of the station buildings have long gone. Here Stanier '8F' 2-8-0 No. 48744 is seen shunting ballast wagons in the up sidings in February 1966. These sidings were in constant use in the early years of this century when stone from the quarries above Padley (destined for the construction of nearby Howden and Derwent dams) was brought by rope-worked incline to a point just out of sight to the left of the picture.

certainly not easy to get good pictures of moving trains and it is not surprising that many of my early exposures are portraits of locomotives on shed. Technically, many are of an acceptable standard, but few, if any, are of anything more than casual interest today. On the other hand, the few which show the setting and the layout of the shed in addition to the loco are prized.

My interest in railway photography continues to this day but it is a very different hobby compared with 30 years ago. Today, steam activity on the main line is still fairly limited and photography can often involve several hundred miles of travel to secure just a few exposures. So often the choice of location is a compromise between gradient, wind direction, local vegetation, other enthusiast photographers and the time the train is expected to pass. How different it was in the days of real steam; the prime philosophy then was to let the trains come to you rather than the other way round. A day's photography often involved just a fifteen-mile stretch of line, and locations could be varied as the position of the sun altered. Indeed, photography was a sufficiently relaxed pastime to allow a pint at the local

at lunch time - after all, this was the time when the sun was at its highest and least amenable, in theory, to good pictures. I also remember sacrificing a whole day's photography at Scout Green on Shap to help a motorist recover his car from a moorland ditch.

My great regret of that period was that in spite of the fact there was so much to photograph, the tendency was to visit the same places time and time again. Well, which would you have selected if it was a choice of Widnes, Warrington or Shap? I tend to forget too that at this time there was a plethora of other transport goodies to photograph. A number of towns – Wolverhampton and Bournemouth, to name but two – were still operating trolley buses, while the number of steam locomotives in industrial service ran into thousands rather than hundreds. There were even a few places where the enthusiast could still find steam-powered lorries at work.

One of the nicer aspects of the hobby in the 1960s was that at the start of a day's photography you didn't really know exactly what you were going to see. Remember, these were the days before TOPS (Total Operations Processing System). That Bradford Forster Square-Carlisle local could produce a 'Jubilee', a 'Black Five', a 'Clan' or even an Ivatt 'Mogul'.

I admire the work of today's preservationists – the railway world is much the richer for them – but sadly, no matter how they struggle to recreate a little of the past I fear the glorious years have gone forever. The line-up of evening suburban trains at Liverpool Street, the atmosphere of Mexborough shed late on a Sunday as engines are prepared for work on Monday, the parade of summer Saturday holiday trains along the sea wall at Dawlish… Does anyone have a good time machine for sale?

Holbeck shed in Leeds has a special place in my memories of the steam era. Along with Doncaster, and to a lesser extent Crewe, this was where I spent many of my youthful Saturdays. Holbeck and Neville Hill were always sheds 'to do' during a day's visit, although Stourton and Copley Hill were rarely on our list of priorities. At Holbeck, there was always the prospect of 'bagging' a rare Polmadie or Kingmoor 'Jubilee'. Getting access to the roundhouse was far from easy. The official entrance took you right past the gaffer's office and one of the unofficial ways in, through one of the windows seen in this picture, required the antics of a midget contortionist. However, this picture was taken with the blessing of the shed foreman. A delightfully grimy 'Jubilee' class 4-6-0 No. 45573 *Newfoundland* poses on the turntable in June 1965.

R. C. Riley

I was born and brought up in Tulse Hill, at that time a relatively upmarket suburb of South London. We had three parks within easy reach and an Irish Terrier that needed a good deal of walking. Two of the parks had railway lines nearby. Walking to Dulwich Park took us along a footpath from West Dulwich station to the Union Bridge near Sydenham Hill, and here I saw 'Lord Nelson' class 4-6-0s on Continental expresses such as the 'Golden Arrow' and 'King Arthurs' on Kent coast trains. Slightly further was Tooting Bec Common where the former LBSCR main line out of Victoria could be observed with its 'Baltic' tanks, 'Atlantics' and other handsome Brighton engines. The United Dairies had a large bottling plant in Valley Road, Streatham, and since neither of the Streatham stations had adequate facilities, Tulse Hill was the railhead for this traffic, at that time carried in churns. The milk trains were usually handled by 0-6-2 tanks, while the local freight was in charge of Class 'C2' 0-6-0s.

At the age of nine I became a season ticket holder and travelled daily to Holborn Viaduct to attend Mercers School. Now just a distant memory, Herne Hill sorting sidings was a busy place, while Holborn Viaduct handled all the parcels traffic, brought in or taken out by horse-drawn carts. With the LNER (GN) 0-6-2Ts, 0-6-0Ts and LMS (MR) 0-6-0Ts bursting out of Snow Hill tunnel, the combination of smoke (especially 'Barnsley Hards' used on the former GNR engines) and horse manure made Holborn Viaduct quite the smelliest station in London. As I grew older (and pocket money increased!) I could visit some of the northern lines' London termini. From 1934 I used to take the bus from Tulse Hill to Euston and watch the dwindling numbers of former LNWR 4-4-0s and 4-6-0s. The following year after school I would take the tram down Grays Inn Road to King's Cross to see the 5.30pm departure of the 'Silver Jubilee'.

By this time my father had given me a Box Brownie which he acquired through cigarette coupons (fortunately he later gave up smoking and lived to the age of 89). My first attempt at railway photography was at King's Cross, the Gresley 'Pacific' *Solario* backing out of the platform. At 1/25 second it was hopeless! I did get some better photographs at Euston, but in 1937 I acquired from an uncle a Kodak folding camera which had speeds of up to 1/100 second,

good enough for locomotive portraits, but still inadequate for moving trains. At the end of 1938 I joined the staff of Glyn Mills & Co, Bankers in Lombard Street. With the rumblings of Munich the bank coerced all its juniors to join the Territorial Army, when its strength was doubled in April 1939. Hence in September as war was declared I was in the Army. Initially we guarded what were known as 'vulnerable points' such as Tower Bridge. The most interesting place was Northolt Aerodrome, which had the GW & GC joint line running beside it. Despite the blackout, powerful torches could be bought, and at one airport location beside the line I used one to advantage to see the GW '47XX' class 2-8-0s and a variety of LNER engines on the night freights. These were the months of the 'phoney war' and I was never found out, despite occasional, sometimes colourful, admonitions from drivers.

One of the sergeants sold me a Foth Derby miniature camera which took negatives marginally larger than 35mm. He knew it was no good, as I found out, but it fitted nicely in a battle dress pocket. Being a non-standard film, supplies very quickly dried up. I do recall using it in bad light from the subway

GWR '14XX' class 0-4-2T No. 1471 on the 10.26am Exeter-Dulverton train pauses at Bampton (Devon), so named in the timetable as there was a like-named station in Oxfordshire. This was on July 3 1963, when the Exe Valley line had only three more months of life, but passengers can still be seen alighting. The cutting in which the station was situated has now been totally infilled and it is possible to pass without realising that there had ever been a station there. There is one clue – the houses above the cutting on the down side are in Station Road. As the branch closed, No. 1471 was also withdrawn from traffic in October 1963.

below Wolverhampton High Level overlooking the GWR station when a 'Dean Goods' with WD 176 markings appeared. Within two minutes I was moved on by a Transport policeman, but fortunately the camera was hidden! In 1943 I transferred to Royal Engineers Railway Operating at Longmoor and it is a matter of regret that I could not take photographs. Quite irregularly, I took the old Kodak out to Normandy in 1944 and recorded some French locomotives at Bayeux. Later I came to record Belgian locomotives, since my duties at a transportation spares depot took me all over the country. A large number of these photographs has been published in Belgian steam books. One classic misprint in a British book depicted a damaged steam tram engine and shed at Venlo, Holland allegedly in August 1944. Had this been the case there would have been no stalag for me, it would have meant a firing squad! In fact, the photograph was taken in April 1946.

After demobilisation I acquired an Agfa Speedex camera, still inadequate for my needs since its top speed was 1/250 second, but it served me for a few years. Apart from the disastrous miniature camera, I had remained faithful to 2$\frac{1}{4}$in x 3$\frac{1}{4}$in negatives. In 1950 I bought a secondhand Zeiss Ikonta, still with only a shutter speed of 1/250 second. At this time I was more concerned with travelling over all surviving WR lines open to passengers. This was virtually completed in the summer of 1951, when with the aid of a monthly return from Paddington to Aberystwyth (£3 3s. 11d. or £3.20!) I travelled out via Shrewsbury and back via Carmarthen. Incidentally, on this trip I visited my last three main WR engine sheds: Birkenhead, Brecon and Neyland. In 16

With a light layer of cloud obscuring the sun, this was the view from Burlescombe signalbox, September 4 1954, as 'Grange' class 4-6-0 No. 6867 *Peterston Grange* tackled the last mile of the climb to Whiteball summit with the Saturdays-only 11am Newquay-York. The engine would have taken over haulage of the train at Plymouth and its grimy condition suggests that it had spent most of the previous week on freight duties from Pontypool Road, its home shed. Had the sun not been obscured this view would not have been possible.

days, including the early August Bank Holiday (which enabled me to reach Barry Pier) I travelled over 1,944½ miles at a cost of £9 13s. 4½d. (£9.68). Those were the days! Two months later I made another lengthy journey. BR had announced that from 1952 fares by former competitive routes would be charged on a mileage basis. However, in 1951 it was still possible to travel from Euston to Swansea, via Shrewsbury, for the same fare as the shorter journey from Paddington. I duly presented myself at Euston and asked for a monthly return to Swansea. The booking clerk laughed – customer care was a long way off then – 'You've come to the wrong station, mate,' he said. I quickly disillusioned him and he looked at me with new respect as he presented me with the ticket. 'You're going to get your moneysworth,' he said, to which I replied, 'That is the idea!' In fact I never went to Shrewsbury. I broke my journey at Wellington to take advantage of the sparse service of the Much Wenlock to Craven Arms line, then about to be closed.

Since the editor has asked me to submit only West Country photographs for this book it is relevant to note that from 1954 to 1963 inclusive my main summer holiday was always spent in Somerset, Devon or Cornwall. In 1955 I acquired a secondhand Agfa Isolette taking 2¼in square negatives. The following year I replaced it with a new model, but not for long, as in October 1956 there was a limited import of Agfa Record II cameras with f4.5 lens and speeds to 1/500 second, the same specification as the Isolettes. However, I was now back to 2¼ x 3¼in negatives, my preferred size. Moreover, in 1954,

It seldom happens that the railway photographer is able to include two moving trains in one picture. One such occasion was at Plymouth North Road, July 4 1957, as the up 'Cornishman', 10.30am Penzance-Wolverhampton (Low Level) was leaving the station. In charge was 'County' class 4-6-0 No. 1010 *County of Caernarvon* and the train consisted of BR Mark 1 coaches with a GWR restaurant car all in chocolate and cream livery. On the right the station pilot, '4575' class 2-6-2T No. 5506 heads towards the station under the control of a shunt signal. Also to be seen is SR Class 'N' 2-6-0 No. 31830 on a down freight to Plymouth Friary.

'King' class 4-6-0 No. 6029 was built in August 1930 as *King Stephen*, the last of its class. On the death of King George V it was renamed *King Edward VIII* in May 1936. On that monarch's abdication No. 6028 became *King George VI* in January 1937. No. 6029 was in charge of the normally heavily loaded 6.25am Penzance-Paddington on the well-known stretch of coastline between Teignmouth and Dawlish. It was recorded on July 1 1957, a Monday, when the load was only nine corridors, an easy task for a 'King'. Still in single chimney form it was fitted with a double chimney in December 1957, by which time only seven 'Kings' remained to be so fitted. It was withdrawn and broken up in April 1962.

Class '74XX' 0-6-0PT stands at Chard Central station, July 6 1961, with the 12.06pm train for Chard Junction. The train had arrived earlier from Taunton, where the engine was based. It was fortuitous that there happened to be flat trucks standing at the spot from which I wished to take the photograph. I have arranged a few things in the course of my photography, but this was not one of them – pure chance. The Chard branch closed during the following year and the only GWR overall roof surviving at a country station is that at Frome.

I had been admitted to the select band of railway photographers that made up Maurice Earley's Railway Photographic Society. Prior to this I had all my work professionally processed, sometimes with dire results. Now I was developing my own films and making my own enlargements. Having a good negative to start with by exercising care in the developing stage, made a great difference. At that time I used Ilford FP3 film, usually developed in Promicrol. It was a great breakthrough to be in the Railway Photographic Society, enabling me to submit prints in portfolios and have them criticised by some of the greatest names in railway photography. This was the greatest advance in my photography I could ever have wished for.

I always liked being above my subject, if possible, from an overbridge, from a signal box, if I could gain entry, or from a signal post with the permission of any local railwayman if there was one present. Those were free and easy days before the coming of the Health & Safety Executive. I remember once being perched on the Princetown branch starter at Yelverton while my companion talked with the porter, who remarked, 'I hope your mate isn't going to be up there for long, my guv'nor's due back in a few minutes and he is a bit militant!' This was a standing joke with Ivo Peters, with whom I was later destined to make many lineside expeditions. In 1954 Alan Pegler was a director of BR Eastern Region and in September he organised a remarkable special train for fellow members of the Royal Observer Corps from Leeds to Farnborough for the Air Show. Motive power was provided by ex-GNR 4-4-2 No. 251, out of the old York Railway Museum, and ex-GC

'Director' class 4-4-0 No. 62663 *Prince Albert*. Ivo Peters had driven O. S. Nock down to see the train and then went on to Basingstoke shed to record the engines being serviced. It was a glorious September day, with low sun, and there were many photographers present. The story that Ivo Peters used to enjoy telling was this:

O. S. Nock: 'Have you ever met Dick Riley?'
Ivo Peters: 'No, I haven't had that pleasure.'
O. S. Nock: 'There he is on top of that lighting mast.'

Thus we met! Nobody could fail to get good photographs that day and the SR contributed to the interest with Urie 'Arthur' and 'Remembrance' 4-6-0s. Frustrated with not having the ability to take colour photographs on such an occasion, I bought a 35mm Agfa Silette the very next day – a true case of 'locking the stable door after the horse has bolted'. In those days the film speed of Kodachrome film was 8ASA, and with a f3.5 lens the maximum shutter speed that could be used was 1/100 second. No use for lineside work, but it would have been ideal in Basingstoke shed that day!

Thus started in a small way my colour photography, but it was not until the

There was a steady climb from Taunton to Whiteball and this grew worse in the four miles from Wellington, at which point very heavy trains would pause for a banking engine. Even with a 13-coach load, 'Castle' class 4-6-0 No. 5059 *Earl St Aldwyn* had managed without assistance. It was recorded breasting the summit past Whiteball Siding signalbox with the Saturday 11.25am Cardiff-Penzance. In the siding is Class '41XX' 2-6-2T No. 4136 which had provided banking assistance for the previous train. The fireman had visited the signalbox to enquire when there would be a likely path for it to return to Wellington.

I was driving to Yelverton to catch a train on the scenic Princetown branch on July 5 1955 when I spotted this location not far from the station. I realised that it would be suitable to record the 10.40am Plymouth-Tavistock South. As it was slowing for the station stop I chanced the limited shutter speed of 1/100 second. The engine was No. 5572, among the last five of the small 2-6-2Ts to be built, in February 1929. The first 75 of the class, built between 1906 and 1924, had a smaller water capacity. With 4ft 7°in driving wheels these engines had a remarkable turn of speed. No. 5572 was one of fifteen fitted for push and pull work in the Cardiff Valleys in 1953, but five years later had been displaced by dieselisation and was transferred to Plymouth Laira. Withdrawn in April 1962 it survived sale to Woodhams at Barry and was rescued and restored by the Great Western Society at Didcot.

In one of the early GWR publications there was a picture of a 'Star' on a down express at Exeter St Davids, taken from a great height. Since I liked being above my subject I identified the location in 1962 as a large water tank with adequate steps to reach the top. Access to the engine shed was over the level crossing east of the station and I followed a British Transport policeman at a respectful distance until he returned to the platform. The resulting photograph on June 23 1962 was of SR Class 'Z' 0-8-0T No. 30957 banking a Bulleid 'Pacific'-hauled train up the 1-in-37 gradient to Exeter Central. The 0-8-0Ts replaced the dainty little Maunsell-rebuilt Stroudley 0-6-2Ts of Class 'E1/r' in 1959, to be succeeded in turn by Class 'W' 2-6-4Ts in 1962.

spring of 1955 that I could really make use of the new medium. This camera was replaced in June 1957 when a limited import of Agfa Silette cameras with f2 Solagon lenses became available. This enabled me at least to use 1/250 second, so colour photography of trains had to be in the vicinity of stations, on adverse gradients or on branch lines. This excellent camera served me for ten years, to be eventually replaced in 1967 by a Canon SLR camera. My most prolific black and white photography was carried out in the years 1955-60. With the end of steam on the Southern Region in 1967 I ceased taking black and white photographs. While my colour output had gradually increased there were two developments. Notably, in September 1961 a new emulsion Kodachrome 2 replaced the original Kodachrome. This had a speed of 25ASA but initially its colour quality did not match the original, although now, years later, it has been totally improved. I did not use Kodachrome 64 ASA because when it first came out it tended to be highly contrasty and grainy. The other factor that affected my photography was that not only was the steam locomotive disappearing from the scene, but also the survivors were often in a dirty uncared-for condition and this did not make for good colour results. I preferred photographing the train in its environment rather than just the train. This medium can be carried on with modern traction photography, but apart from a few shots in the early days I have never really adapted to this subject.

William John Verden Anderson

Born March 28 1932
Died September 23 1989

A tribute by Brian Stephenson

Opposite Reid North British Railway 'Scott' class 'D30' 4-4-0 No. 62426 *Cuddie Headrigg* departs from the former Caledonian Railway Edinburgh Princes Street terminus with the 5.22pm stopping train to Stirling via Polmont on May 14 1956. It was allocated to the former CR shed at Stirling, and survived until June 1960 when it had completed almost 46 years of service having been built at Cowlairs in 1914. The station itself did not last a great deal longer, being closed in September 1965 when traffic was diverted to Edinburgh Waverley, the former North British station. This photograph was taken with Bill's Newman & Guardia camera using 2½in x 3½in HP3 plates, which he used for all his classic photographs between 1954 and 1964.

W. J. Verden Anderson, 'Bill' as he was known to all, was born in Edinburgh, the eldest son of Eric Anderson, senior partner in the paper-making business of Smith, Anderson & Company based at Leslie, Fife. He was raised in the family house overlooking the Fettykil Paper Mill in the valley below, where he would have been able to gaze down on the daily goods train from Markinch, as the usual NBR Class 'J37' 0-6-0 shunted the sidings at the mill, bringing coal for the boilers and taking finished paper and empties away. Although he never mentioned to the writer that this nurtured his interest in railways he often likened the paper-making machines to steam locomotives, for they conveyed to him a similar impression of speed and grandeur, although on an even larger scale.

He was sent to Rugby School as a boarder and as he revealed in his 'Glorious Years' feature in the first issue of *Steam World,* he was inveigled into his first afternoon of train spotting by one of the boys in his class. Rugby, on the West Coast main line with the Great Central crossing over on a great viaduct about a quarter of a mile south of the station, was a busy location in the late 1940s and it was here that the 'official' spotting point was. He was soon fascinated by the railway, but quickly recognised the futility of just watching the trains and was soon taking photographs of them with the inevitable family box camera.

He had the great good fortune to have the Rev. A. W. V. Mace as School Chaplain, who was also a skilled railway photographer in his own right. Bill received considerable encouragement and tuition in the rudiments of darkroom work from Arthur Mace, and in 1949 he was guided into purchasing a second-hand Voigtlander Bessa III 120-size folding camera with a less than perfect Voigtar lens for the then huge sum of £10. With this camera Bill took a number of quite good photographs around Rugby and on his home lines in Fife. He

Bill Anderson was attracted to the former Caledonian main line between Carlisle and Glasgow where there was considerable variety of traffic and locomotives. Here rebuilt 'Royal Scot' class 4-6-0 No. 46105 *Cameron Highlander* from Polmadie shed, Glasgow, tackles the ten-mile climb to Beattock summit with a Manchester Victoria-Glasgow Central express near Harthope in July 1961. A plume of steam can be seen at the rear of the train coming from the banking engine taken on at Beattock for the climb. This would usually be an LMS 2-6-4T at this date but occasionally a CR 0-4-4T was still used. The gradients on the climb to Beattock summit average between 1-in-74 to 1-in-88 with a short length of 1-in-69.

had his first railway photographs published while still at school with a view of the last Highland 'Loch' 4-4-0 in the June 1950 issue of *Trains Illustrated,* followed the next month by a shot of a freight train on the Great Central just south of Rugby.

During his National Service in the RAF Bill was fortunate to be posted to Kinloss, and this gave him the opportunity to explore the local lines with the aid of his trusty cycle. He took several photographs with the Voigtlander camera on the Speyside line out of Craigellachie as well as on the local Elgin-Forres line. Traffic on these lines was very light, so careful planning was required to get to the right spot in time and he cycled some considerable distances. When at home he photographed trains on the Edinburgh-Dundee main line that passed within a few miles of his home at Lochmuir summit and around Thornton Junction. He took his camera with him on many other journeys and thus we have a few photographs taken in Plymouth and Cornwall, as well as in Norway and Sweden.

By now Bill was finding the old Voigtlander far from satisfactory, as the writer can testify from experience in printing some of the negatives taken with it. Bill had been admitted to Maurice Earley's Railway Photographic Society when he was only 20 and through the Society made contact with Eric Treacy

who advised him on the purchase of a Newman & Guardia 3½in x 2½in plate camera with a Ross Xpres lens. It was with this camera that some of the finest pictures of Scotland's railways were taken, including all but two in this feature on his work.

He started using the plate camera in the spring of 1954 and within a week of its purchase he took a photograph that won him first prize in the 1954 *Trains Illustrated* photographic competition. Needless to say this spurred him on and a whole series of superb images were taken in the next ten years. He used Ilford HP3 plates, which had a superb tonal range but sadly do not give the best definition when blown-up really large. Bill's technique was to set the train in its surroundings, often carefully using trees, signals or even telegraph poles to help frame the photograph. He did this is in such a way that his pictures became instantly recognisable, the credit line under his pictures merely confirming what the reader had already guessed. He was described by David Wilcock in *Steam Railway* at the time of his untimely death 'as perhaps the most inspirational of all railway cameramen in the post-war steam era; his pictures of steam in the Highland and lowland landscapes had such a definitive hallmark of quality, clarity and balance of composition, that they were immediately recognisable as Anderson pictures'.

Until the end of steam in Scotland the Anderson plate camera ranged over

Almost at the end of steam working in Scotland an evening Class 'H' goods train for Dundee sets out from Perth behind a grimy Thompson LNER Class 'B1' 4-6-0 on the single-line bridge over the River Tay to Barnhill in summer 1966. Thomas Telford's elegant road bridge, in the background, makes an interesting contrast with the more recent railway structure, which, together with the 'Fair City' – former ancient capital of Scotland – the river and the mountains, amounts to a classic picture brought to life by the steam train in the middle. The photograph was taken with Bill's Linhof roll film press camera, acquired in 1964, using Tri-X film.

What a splendid sight LMS 'Princess Coronation' class 4-6-2 No. 46241 *City of Edinburgh* makes as it storms south out of Perth with the thirteen-coach 8.50pm sleeping car express for Euston in July 1960. The train is taking the curve of the former Caledonian main line at Hilton Junction as the locomotive is working hard on the three miles of slightly downgrade and level track before starting the eleven-mile climb to Gleneagles. The 'Pacific', from Crewe North shed, will be working through to its home town. The long summer evenings in Scotland enabled Bill to photograph such a dramatic scene, but in winter, photography was curtailed due to the much shorter days.

One of the ten McIntosh-designed Caledonian 0-4-4Ts built for the LMS in 1925, No. 55263 brings the one carriage 4.05pm school train from Callander to Killin up the long 1-in-60 gradient from Balquhidder through the dramatic Glen Ogle in May 1960. This train would work the five-mile branch service from Killin Junction to Killin, making the journey to Callander to bring the children home during term time. The line was permanently closed in September 1965 after a rock fall near this spot, but was due to close under the Beeching plan a few weeks later with the through Oban trains being diverted over the former North British route south of Crianlarich.

most of the country, occasionally down to Shap, but seldom elsewhere, except to Norway and Sweden where he was sent on business when he joined the family paper-making concern after completing his National Service. It was in Sweden that he met his wife Birgitta. After work at the paper mill he would often dash out in summer if the weather was fine, now driving his Morris 1000 or Sunbeam Rapier, either to a spot between Mawcarse Junction and Glenfarg to photograph the 4.05pm Edinburgh-Perth (which he photographed at the same spot no fewer than 25 times – see picture of No. 60011), or over to the climb out of Markinch to Lochmuir Summit for the 4.15pm Edinburgh-Aberdeen express, both trains normally 'Pacific' hauled. In later years when diesels appeared he would go further to Perth for the departure of the 4.45pm fish train to the south which often had a Stanier 'Pacific' or 'Britannia' at its head.

At holiday times he would usually go to the Highlands, taking many memorable photographs on the West Highland, Callander & Oban line and Highland line proper. Pictures at large stations such as the view at Edinburgh Princes Street were exceedingly few, much to his regret in later years when the whole steam age infrastructure was disappearing. The total number of photographs taken with the plate cameras, for he acquired a Zeiss Contessa Nettel around 1961, was only 1,800 – not a large number by today's standards. He did acquire another roll film camera during this period, but it was used only very sparingly and probably only when the plate camera was out of action or he had run out of plates or holders to put them in. This latter point was a great drawback, as you had to have not only a dark holder for each exposure, but also access to a suitable place of total darkness in which to reload. This was fine when working from home, but not very convenient on extended photographic outings. However, Bill took a changing bag and portable developing tank with which he could, and did, develop a single plate at the lineside. This was a somewhat risky business, but was justified in his eyes as he could check out the results before taking any more shots at that particular location.

Towards the end of 1963, getting a regular supply of glass plates was becoming difficult and the plate cameras were getting older, so Bill sought a replacement in the form of a Linhof 6x7 press camera which took 120-size roll film. Derek Cross had been using a similar camera for some years and I think it was this that prompted Bill to purchase one, but the camera was somewhat over-engineered and proved unreliable though it lasted until 1972. Some 800 pictures were taken with it, some very good, particularly from longer-distance viewpoints. Normally he used Kodak Tri-X film developed in D76, which he found had better definition and finer grain than the old HP3 plates or film. The Linhof camera was replaced in 1972 by one of the then brand new Pentax 6x7 120-size roll film cameras. In a letter written to me in 1976 he says, 'As far as I can see, the Pentax 6x7 is the answer to the railway photographer's prayer. What a tragedy we did not have such a machine years ago.' In fact he used the 6x7 camera and a second one for the rest of his life, taking many superb colour transparencies with it as well as black and white.

During his National Service, Bill Anderson was posted to RAF Kinloss, where he was able to photograph trains on the local Forres-Elgin line and also at Craigellachie for the former Great North of Scotland lines. Here one of the Pickersgill GNSR Class 'D40' 4-4-0s No. 62265, built in 1909 at the Company's own workshops at Inverurie, heads away from Craigellachie on the idyllic Speyside line with the two-carriage morning train for Boat of Garten early in 1952. Note the snow plough fitted beneath the buffer beam as insurance against the possibility of inclement weather. This is the only photograph in this selection of Bill's work taken with the Voigtlander Bessa III camera.

As steam in Scotland and England declined, Bill started travelling further afield visiting the lines around North and South Blyth, Consett, making a first visit with his camera to the Settle & Carlisle line, and even managing a single trip to the Isle of Wight. He also teamed up with Derek Cross for a couple of days' photography in south-west Scotland. It was with Derek that he produced the two volumes of *Steam in Scotland*, the only books to date containing a large collection of his photographs. I was, by this time, a member of the Railway Photographic Society and had a reputation for producing fine quality print. This had not gone unnoticed by Bill and he asked me if I could take on the job of making prints from his plates and negatives for the books. In the event, I came to edit the second volume and we became friends. Sadly, Bill never found time to produce any more books of his work.

The last of the traditional 'Anderson' lines was the Killin branch, which Bill visited several times towards the end of its life in 1965 and, while doing so, came across a derelict water mill at Balquhidder, which he purchased and set about restoring as a holiday home for his growing family, even to the extent of getting the water wheel turning once again. Bill and Birgitta's family grew to six – Katrina, Graeme, Anna, Veronica, Susie and finally Keith, who was born after steam on BR had finished but who spent many happy hours out with his father in the last years of his life photographing diesels on the Highland lines and elsewhere.

After steam had finished in Scotland, and with increasing commitment to business and family, Bill became chairman of the family firm and an acknowledged expert in the business of papermaking. He had developed a recycled paper under the 'TreeSaver' brand name some 25 years ago, long before the current environmental pressure to do so. The firm had also expanded into polythene bag manufacture in the late 1960s and remains to this day one of the largest paper-bag makers. For Bill, railway photography became mainly a holiday occupation and he made numerous visits to countries where steam was still in operation.

Gresley Class 'A4' 4-6-2 No. 60011 *Empire of India* climbs the slightly rising gradient between Mawcarse Junction and Glenfarg with the 4.05pm Edinburgh Waverley-Perth during 1957. This train was never sure about its status, often carrying a Class 'B' headlamp code as it stopped at most stations, but it was normally hauled by a Haymarket 'Pacific'. In the mountainous background is the West Lomond Hill, one of the 'Paps of Fife'. This was one of Bill's favourite photographic locations to which he would hurriedly dash after work to photograph the two evening trains, the other being the 4.35pm from Glasgow usually hauled by a 4-4-0. Sadly, this part of the line has long been buried beneath the tarmac of the M90 motorway.

A country which Bill became particularly fond of was Portugal to which he made several visits. I particularly remember his excitement when he returned from a visit in June 1970 after he had found a particularly spectacular location along the Douro Valley east of Tua and had brought back a photo of a broad-gauge compound 4-6-0, which he regarded as a master shot. When asked he would not reveal how to reach this location! While steam lasted in Europe he also visited Austria, France, Finland, Germany, Spain and Switzerland and went on to photograph in South Africa, South America and India; he also revisited Norway and Sweden for some of the museum lines. During the 1980s he became more active in the UK, photographing preserved operations and, increasingly, the current BR scene in Scotland.

When Bill realised he was terminally ill he made arrangements for all his black and white plates and negatives to be put into my care as he knew I could turn out prints to the standard he expected in his photographs. Also, the fact that I had already set up Rail Archive Stephenson meant that I had the contacts to ensure that his photographs continued to appear in books and magazines as was his wish and not allow them to be buried far from view in some national archive or other. One very great difficulty with the Anderson legacy is the fact that he did not keep any details of where or when his photographs were taken. Much information has been collected by trawling through all the various books and publications in which his photographs have appeared, and by my personal knowledge of the collection.

With Bill Anderson's death in September 1989 at the early age of 57, after a courageous three-year fight against cancer, Scotland lost the finest railway photographer it is ever likely to know. I lost a railway photographer friend who, in his modest way, set an example to all who take up this rewarding hobby.

My grateful thanks go to Bill's widow Birgitta and to his youngest son, Keith, and indeed to all the Anderson family for their help and friendship.

On the Highland main line two miles north of Carr Bridge, Pickersgill Caledonian Railway '72' class 4-4-0 No. 54482, built at St Rollox in 1920, and Stanier LMS Class '5' 4-6-0 No. 44924, toil up the 1-in-60/70 gradient on the five-mile climb to Slochd summit (1,315ft) with a northbound train of locomotive coal for Inverness motive power depot. The train has already surmounted the 16-mile climb to Druimauchdar summit (1,484ft). This scene gives some idea of what it must have been like during the First World War when numerous trains of steam coal had to be worked to the far north for the fleet at Scapa Flow, often using run-down inadequate motive power.

Ben Ashworth

Opposite Below the town of Cinderford and at the heart of the GWR Forest of Dean rail system and original tramway junction network, was Bilson Junction. As late as 1965, less than two years before complete closure, three short branches remained in use, diverging from Bilson yard. This scene was recorded on July 22 1965 from the site of an overbridge originally carrying the Severn & Wye Railway into Cinderford town. GWR 0-6-0PT No. 8729 will have used an appreciable amount of water slogging up 1-in-50 gradients through the Forest from Severnside at Bullo Pill, so the tanks are topped up at Bilson Junction North before propelling empties up to the Northern United colliery. This colliery was the last deep mine belonging to the NCB in the Forest of Dean and closed at Christmas in 1965.

Like many others with an interest in railways, railway photography came as a fairly natural progression from the childhood hobby of recording engine numbers, which in my case started in the middle of the 1939-45 war.

What an interesting time that was! With none of the wartime worries that concerned the adults, many hours were spent down at nearby Coaley Junction station, in Gloucestershire, absorbed in logging the passage of wartime freight, troop trains, ambulance trains, locomotives from the USA and Austerity 2-10-0 and 2-8-0 engines of home manufacture, not to mention occasional rarities from depots in the distant north. Besides main line traffic, there were long spells of shunting goods generated by the $2^1/_2$-mile branch line to Dursley. The branch passed within a stone's throw (just) of home, so railways were a part of my everyday life – small wonder that some fifteen years later I should feel the need to record such familiar scenes before they vanished for ever. Having said this, I think a conscious effort usually has to be made to record the commonplace, and often it's not until a familiar scene has gone that one realises it is too late. Even now I still have occasional strangely distorted dreams of rather improbable train movements on that long-vanished branch line. They are usually photographically frustrating – trees in the way, and so on!

It was another lad at school (he later spent most of his adult life working for Rhodesian Railways) who set off my recording of numbers of locomotives on the Gloucester-Bristol main line, which was an outpost of the former Midland Railway. When monochrome film reappeared after the war he took up photography, but I considered it too complicated a subject to master and preferred to spend my pocket money on travel. I already had a leaning towards railways as a result of long train journeys to summer camping holidays in what at that time were far-flung places such as the west coasts of Ireland and Scotland. These train journeys were long-anticipated and, though I didn't realise it at the time, probably helped towards an appreciation of the passing scene and of the railway's place in its surroundings. In 1936 we camped in west Wales near Barmouth and en route I was given a copy of Heath Robinson's *Railway Ribaldry;* I still remember my fascination with his ingeniously quaint illustrations, in particular those of railway byways. Later in life, it was always

the remoter parts of a railway network that interested me most.

By the summer of 1947 I had acquired my first bicycle and one of my elder sisters gave me her pre-war Kodak box camera with eight exposures on 120 film which was used with reasonable success in the Black Country, Shrewsbury and Crewe on summer holiday railway expeditions. Photographic highlights for me were snapping an LNWR 0-8-0 at 3B shed yard, Bushbury, the last LNWR 'Claughton' in 3A shed yard, Bescot, *Duchess of Gloucester* from the wooden footbridge at Crewe and *Princess Elizabeth*, ex-works, also at Crewe and waiting to take over an up express.

The camera was then more or less forgotten about.

In 1948 I was called up for national service and, mostly at the army's expense, was pulled by 30 different ex-GW, LMS and SR locomotives on journeys to destinations between north Wales and south-east England before being despatched to the Far East. I evidently hadn't completely forgotten photography because I made room in a kitbag for the camera. I also managed to carry it on two or three operations in Malaya where journeys to more remote jungle areas with no road access were often by train along the east coast from Gemas; traction by courtesy of the North British Locomotive Company. A few reasonable railway photographs were secured in spite of various problems, one being that film, once out of its cannister, would stick together overnight in the high humidity. Although the camera survived torrential rain at various times and a river crossing inside a waterproof bag, I reluctantly abandoned it in Singapore when the film transport jammed halfway through a film. Fortunately this disappointment came only a couple of months before returning

Trains leaving Gloucester's Eastgate and Central stations converged on Horton Road level crossing, and loco movements in and out of Horton Road shed yard could also be seen by standing on the crossbar of a bicycle propped against the fence. That is how this scene was photographed on September 21 1964. A GWR 2-8-0 was a pretty tight fit in the available space and a slightly higher viewpoint would have been nice, especially as vans or lorries frequently stopped in the foreground, so blocking the view. On the left is the GWR loco shed and to the right, Tramway Junction signal box, named after the Cheltenham-Gloucester tramway which passed through this location 30 years before the railway arrived.

On April 21 1965, shunting had finished for the morning at Nailsworth, a tea can was handed down and the BR class 2 left to simmer while the crew had their meal break. Judging from the spectators it was the school Easter holiday, as the Stroud/ Nailsworth trip only ran three times a week and not on Saturdays. Now a housing estate, the terminus of the Midland Railway branch at Nailsworth was unusual, with a split-level approach. The picturesque station building was at a higher level than the large goods yard, cattle pens and Station Hotel.

to the UK, by which time I had already succeeded in recording the oldest and most recently built 4-6-2s, in addition to some Japanese (presumably re-gauged) leftovers dumped at Gemas.

The next venture into photography came when my father loaned me his 1926 Leica 1 (a rare collector's item now) for a couple of cycle tours in 1952 and 1953, by which time colour film was readily available and I was more interested in landscape than railway photography. I could have recorded *Ben Alder* in colour at the side of Inverness shed had I been more enterprising and carried the Leica with me instead of hiding it under my bed in the youth hostel! Highland Railway *Ben Alder* was earmarked for preservation and stored in several places before being 'inadvertently' scrapped.

It wasn't until 1954 when working in Cornwall that I picked up an advertisement by Braun of Nuremberg for a 35mm interchangeable lens Paxette. I sent off a postal order, only to receive a model without interchangeable lens facility. The model advertised was not yet available in the UK. My first lesson in the credibility of advertisers!

That summer my work took me to four RAF airfields in Lincolnshire and Cambridgeshire. Very little film was used on railways, though one brilliantly sunny day I did have a go at the down 'Elizabethan' near Little Bytham using 10ASA Kodachrome. The Paxette only went to 1/300 second and f2.8 so it was hardly an appropriate subject. It would have been far better had I taken an interest in the local east–west traffic passing through the Grantham area, but this was LNER country with 'foreign' motive power which meant little to me,

As a number taker, I knew the Midland Railway roundhouse at Gloucester Barnwood as 22B, but after nationalisation, when the Western Region took over, it became 85E and later 85C before closing in the spring of 1964 when the nearby Horton Road shed took over the servicing of all locos arriving in the Gloucester area. On November 26 1961, a photographic problem was freezing fog, which at intervals drifted across the turntable area. Just visible on the left is the front end of a MR Class '0F' 0-4-0T No. 41535 employed on the extensive network of lines threading the docks in Gloucester. To the right are LMS '4F' 0-6-0 No. 44264, MR '3F' 0-6-0 No. 43645, LMS '8F' 2-8-0 No. 48220 and BR Standard Class '5' 4-6-0 No. 73137. The latter was one of 30 built with Caprotti valve motion, one example of which has survived into preservation.

so I never thought to record any of the older and more interesting locos still pottering around at that time.

Sometime around 1958 a railwayman cycling and walking companion from my home village suggested we went off on a youth hostel expedition combining autumn colour photography with places of railway interest. Twice we explored railways in the Peak District around Buxton and found ourselves in some very interesting terrain. On another occasion we toured south Devon and north Cornwall, were marooned in a flood-bound train, and later cycled down a stretch of the Wenford Bridge china clay branch. Just imagine the furore if such a thing were attempted nowadays! Some useful results on railway subjects were achieved and these were an encouragement to make further attempts closer to home in Gloucestershire. Not long afterwards, it was rumoured that the Upton-on-Severn branch and the MSWJR (Tiddly Dyke) over the Cotswolds were to lose their passenger services. I think it was this as much as anything which finally awakened me to the need for a record to remember it all by. At the time it was difficult to imagine the Cotswolds and the Forest of Dean without their branch and secondary lines, but even before Dr Beeching's recommendations the trend was obviously in that direction. Little did I realise that within a few years 85 per cent of stations and about half the track mileage in Gloucestershire were to disappear – the most interesting half of the network as far as I was concerned. Simultaneously, steam on the Western Region vanished as well, so one way and another it was quite a blow.

Returning to 1960, it very soon became apparent that to get any satisfaction at all with monochrome picture making I would have to attempt my own developing and printing. Around this time Penguin published a book on 'do-it-yourself' photography which proved extremely informative, and, armed with a list of requirements, I bought all the necessary equipment and materials from a local shop, in two stages to spread the financial load. Once I'd got the hang of things, picture quality improved considerably. I discovered the rather expensive (half a crown for 2 fluid ounces) Kodak High Definition Developer and got superb results using it with the Panatomic X at 50ASA. For less bright conditions May & Baker's Promicrol combined very successfully with FP3, and it is only in recent years that I've found anything that will approach the standards set by these long-discontinued developers. In the 1990s, Ilford's XP2, Delta 100 and Delta 400 produce less grainy results, though XP2 is more tricky to develop and lacks the required contrast on some occasions.

From 1961 to the end of Western Region steam my developing tank and enlarger were kept pretty busy, and I was out on every occasion that work, family commitments and weather permitted, concentrating mainly on Gloucestershire railways. A combination of bicycle and train was ideal. The train to get quickly to Ross, Lydney, Chalford, etc., then the cycle for exploring the intricacies of the area in question. Regrettably, this is barely possible on today's railways. Family holidays usually took us somewhere in Wales, preferably with a railway close at hand.

To cope with the increased activity I acquired three secondhand Super Paxettes, two with an f2.8 Tessar and the other with an f2.8 Xenar lens; the latter is now in my enlarger in preference to a 'proper' enlarging lens. I also

This was Gloucester Barnwood shed yard on February 23 1963 and these two gentlemen would have had something decidedly impolite to say had I suggested these were the 'Glorious Years'. Manhandling cold metal in the open with bare hands in the longest and coldest winter since 1740 must have been none too pleasant amongst this clutter and grime. The wheels appear to belong to 'Castle' class 4-6-0 No. 5049 *Earl of Plymouth* lying close by with its centre drivers missing. In May the following year this loco was again in the Gloucester area, dumped with many others on the ex-GWR line connecting the docks with Over Junction. In the background two more railwaymen struggle in the cold dry air with another black and dusty task. Coal tubs, loaded manually from wagons on the coaling stage, are being tipped into the tender of an LMS '4F' 0-6-0.

47

sometimes used a 90mm Wray Plustrar, but the viewfinder slotted into the accessory shoe and was rather a hit-and-miss affair. With three cameras, both slow and fast monochrome film and colour film were available at all times, though it wasn't often that I used colour film on railways, partly because of the expense. As I was reluctant to go out unless the weather looked favourable I got through quite a bit of slow monochrome film, even in the winter. In the late 1960s I bought my first reflex, a Russian Zenit B with a f2 Helios lens. Though heavy and crude, it was quite effective, especially with a secondhand 105mm Pentax lens. I also had a 1958 Russian 37mm lens which I still use now. Then, in the early 1970s I bought a Praktica L for monochrome and an LTL with meter for colour and used them with screw-thread Pentax lenses. Suprisingly, these Prakticas have survived in constant use to the end of 1995, the only addition being a Tamron Adaptall 70-210mm zoom which I always try to use resting against a beanbag or on a support of some kind to do justice to the optics. When the time comes to replace a failed Praktica it could be difficult to find a simple 35mm non-electric camera.

Since the end of BR steam in 1968 I have not often travelled far in this country to see preserved steam, mainline or otherwise. From 1976, however, I have been able to travel overseas and find it refreshing to see something different both scenically and from the railway aspect. Less developed countries in particular allow more freedom to manoeuvre away from the all-too-frequent

A shaft of winter sunshine casts long shadows beneath the ancient GWR canopy at Gloucester Central on February 29 1964. Will it slip? Two pairs of critical eyes turn as BR Standard '9F' 2-10-0 No. 92216, oozing steam, takes the strain on a heavy load of Shell tank wagons from Llandarcy in South Wales. In steam days, north and eastbound trains stopped here to take water and change crews. The seated driver and fireman could easily be waiting to take over an up passenger train. Out of sight on the left is the bay platform for the Chalford auto-train service. In the 1970s this platform was closed and the remaining one lengthened to 1,977ft to accommodate more than one train; during the 1980s it was found necessary to reinstate it.

Viewed from the derelict signal box at Withington in the Cotswolds, this GWR 2-8-0 was on a train recovering sleepers during dismantling of the MSWJR by contractors in the summer of 1963. An earlier train had caused panic amongst workers on an electricity pylon who had temporarily anchored a cable to what they thought was an abandoned stretch of railway line. Fortunately, the engine crew were able to stop short of the obstruction. Immediately after this photograph was taken it became apparent that the track had been slightly slewed towards the platform and there was insufficient clearance to continue safely. The last train ran in September 1961 but, towards the end, Withington station was barely used. In fact, I was accused of trespass in the station approach by a local farmer who didn't realise it was still in the WR timetable.

lineside view, and as for lineside fences and cast iron trespass notices, they are almost non-existent in the countries where steam has survived into the '70s, '80s and '90s.

Inevitably, today's comparatively limited British steam railway photography is a disappointment when compared with former times. There is less freedom to wander without arousing suspicion or annoyance, and the village football match atmosphere which often prevails, with its ranks of orange-uniformed photographers, is not something I want a part in. I had enough of regimentation in the army!

Picking out a dozen or so negatives for this publication was difficult. My own appreciation of a picture can easily be influenced by the difficulties I overcame to reach what I hoped would be an original and worthwhile viewpoint, whereas the casual viewer just accepts the scene on its face value and isn't likely to know or care about the problems involved. In my case it is likely that prints have been made several times before from some negatives, and the novelty has worn off since the results were first seen many years ago. Nostalgia can wear thin on occasion!

Whilst wondering what on earth I could write about photography that would be interesting, it occurred to me that there must be a great many people who

An unpremeditated photograph, taken on December 20 1963, and one of those rare occasions when everything combined to produce a winner first time. I got a shot (not printed until exactly 32 years later!) of the loco taking water at Coleford Junction and then cycled flat out alongside the railway which climbed at a steady 1-in-30/31 for several miles. With a fairly light load behind it I could hear 0-6-0PT No. 4624 slowly gaining on me, so seeing the gap in the trees opposite the pub I dumped the bike and ran for it. An elderly woman came out of the house on the right, mystified by such an unseemly rush. This was a branch of the Severn & Wye Railway which met the Monmouth-Coleford railway, both lines terminating side by side in Coleford town.

aren't aware what a slow, tedious, painstaking business it can be, sitting in a bathroom trying to produce prints showing all the detail and with just the right contrast. I've certainly gained the impression that some publishers don't know or particularly care! For me, the most absorbing part of the process is reconnoitring for viewpoints revealing any outstanding features in a locality. It is a time-consuming occupation, made easier in winter when most trees are bare; and I suspect that 30 years ago there weren't half the number there are now. To avoid attracting unwanted attention I try to remain hidden if possible, although this can produce quite awkward situations. The most unlikely that comes to mind was when I visited the scene of a great railway event a day beforehand to familiarise myself with the surroundings, climbed a tree in order to take photographs over a high wire fence and main line, only to find that two policemen were starting to patrol their respective beat directly below me. I was obliged to remain motionless while they discussed their plan of campaign. Events similar to this have occurred quite a number of times and it was fortunate that on this occasion I hadn't left a camera bag or rucksack at the bottom of the tree. Equipment needs to be camouflaged if left lying around. I have even been forced to climb a tree in order to avoid a line of beaters and dogs

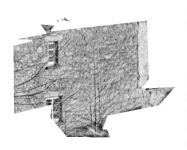

combing a wood for pheasants or deer. A high rock cutting prevented escape across the adjacent railway, though a fox escaped by trotting along the sleepers in the opposite direction from the beaters.

All in all, I suppose railways have provided me with quite an absorbing, if not particularly constructive interest over the last 50 years, as well as an almost unending string of fading memories from past locations and events, outlandish and otherwise.

Right Gas lamps, semaphore signals and a signal box – all long since disappeared, though in 1996 the empty 'T' sidings at Gloucester South were still in place. On May 19 1965, GWR 'Castle' class 4-6-0 No. 5042 *Winchester Castle*, minus nameplates and safety valve bonnet, pulls out of 'T' sidings at sunset with the 8.40pm fitted freight to Old Oak Common. In the mid-1940s *Winchester Castle* was maintained in much better condition to work the Paddington-Cheltenham expresses as far as Gloucester. The signalbox controlled Gloucester South Junction, and in the foreground is the Gloucester avoiding line.

Brian Morrison

Opposite My first lineside permit from Eastern Region was granted in 1951. I had requested that the scope of the permit run from Holloway Bank to Doncaster but what I got was a stretch of line from Hatfield to Hitchin excluding Welwyn viaduct or tunnels! Undeterred I managed to obtain an increase in coverage at renewal the following year – and then in June 1953 the new permit arrived; this time my request had been granted and it included the magic words 'Holloway Bank'. Until I became familiar with the direction of travel on the various lines, the location just north of Copenhagen tunnel was quite a frightening place, but eventually it began to feel quite like home. Away from the tunnel towards Finsbury Park was much more open, but the gradient still produced spectacular exhausts. On September 20 1953, Gresley Class 'A4' 4-6-2 No. 60026 *Miles Beevor* struggles to the summit of the 1-in-107 stretch, hauling a well-laden 11-coach Sunday train from King's Cross with portions for Hull and Bradford Exchange.

Until the age of 12, I had little interest in railways. My adolescent pursuits included cycling, conkers, playing 'Tarzan' in the trees, and collecting cigarette cards. Apart from Uncle Frank, who I later discovered was a staff photographer for the LNER at Liverpool Street, no one in the family was in the railway, and the new school craze of 'engine spotting' held no interest for me. It was a combination of bland school dinners and a greedy prefect in charge of my allocated school dinner table, that finally decided me to ask Mum for a packed lunch. The prefect was not a bully, but he did invoke a sense of injustice in the young Morrison at the way in which he would cut the once-a-week treat of chocolate pudding in half, put one half on his own plate, and then divide the remainder among the five of us unlucky enough to be on his table! At first, the contents of my sandwich box would be eaten in the playing field or in the bike shed if it was raining, but after a time I decided to join the 'spotters' at lunch times and consume my lunch on a pleasant grassy bank at Chislehurst, watching the trains go by. I knew nothing of the different locomotive classes that passed by on the Kent Coast services, but was soon aware that most of the passenger engines and a few of those hauling goods trains carried nameplates. Some were of public schools such as *Eton*, *Dulwich*, *Harrow*, *Rugby* and *Charterhouse*, and in addition there was a variety of roundtable knights from the legend of King Arthur, such as *Sir Ironside*, *Sir Harry le Fise Lake*, the often confused *Sir Balan* and *Sir Balin*, and *Sir Brian* (the latter guaranteed to raise a laugh among my companions when it passed by). These engines were soon augmented by very modern-looking streamliners in green livery with yellow body stripes, which were destined to display nameplates such as *Spitfire*, *Hurricane*, *Anti-Aircraft Command*, *Biggin Hill* and *Winston Churchill*, as well as many of the Kent-based fighter squadrons of the war years.

Some of our gang with more affluent parents now boasted a small printed booklet listing all the engines that we were seeing, and a great many more besides. Some youthful entrepreneurial gathering of wooden boxes from the back of the local fishmonger's shop, which were then chopped into firewood for sale for a few coppers to neighbours (the unsuspecting fishmonger included), augmented

In the 1950s, unless you were fortunate enough to know someone who worked for BR, news was often no longer news by the time one read about it in the magazines of the day, usually some two months later. I was fortunate, therefore, to call in at Clapham Junction on June 23 1951. Waiting on the platform end for the afternoon 'Bournemouth Belle', I was pleasantly surprised when the expected 'Merchant Navy' at the head of the train turned out to be a new 'Britannia' class 'Pacific' No. 70009 *Alfred the Great*. The engine was on loan to the 'Southern' for a very short period and had been temporarily allocated to Stewarts Lane shed.

the meagre proceeds from a paper round, and quickly resulted in acquisition of the Ian Allan *ABC of Southern Locomotives*. Weekend and holiday visits to other lines soon followed, and upon leaving school I decided that I would like to join the railway, if only to gain free travel to pursue my hobby. I never really had any ambition to be an engine driver, and decided that my future would be more of a sedentary one. In those pre-computer times, jobs were fairly easy to come by, and I duly replied to a newspaper advertisement inviting applications for the position of a junior clerk in the Railway Passenger's Assurance Company. After a kindly interview in the City of London, I was taken on – and only later discovered that the company for which I was working was a subsidiary of the large North British & Mercantile Insurance Company (later part of the Commercial Union Group), and had nothing whatever to do with the railways other than to issue baggage tickets to passengers to insure their luggage while on train journeys! Nevertheless the job was quite a pleasant one, and it was while employed there that I met my two lineside friends of the 1950s, Arthur Carpenter and the late Roy Wilson, with whom I spent many enjoyable times over the years.

By the time of my call-up for National Service, I had amassed a reasonable total of underlinings. Nationalisation of the railways now took place – and most of the numbers were altered! The attractive young lady I met while in the Army had rather dimmed my interest in them anyway, and eventually I decided to curtail the pursuit while in khaki, but kept up with what was taking place on the railway scene with monthly copies of both *Railway Magazine* and *Trains Illustrated*. It was in the former that a whole page illustration of a Gresley 'A4' class 'Pacific' climbing Holloway Bank appeared, credited to the photographer J. C. Flemons. It was a striking picture, and it was this that first sparked my interest in the photography of trains. Upon demob I used a modest gratuity from the government of the day to purchase my first camera, and with the balance placed a deposit on an engagement ring; my wife still insists that my priorities went awry somewhere! The camera was an Agfa Isolette 1 with a f4.5 Apotar lens and, most importantly, a Compur Rapid shutter with a top speed marked to 1/500 second. In addition to the photography of moving trains, I set myself the task of trying to obtain a photographic example of every class and sub-class of locomotives then working on British Railways. This was probably the latent spotter coming out in me again, but, nevertheless, it provided a reason for travelling the length and breadth of the country in search of the rarer engines, and even included those on the Isle of Wight system while visiting there on honeymoon! This time my wife accepted the situation, since it was the 10/6d a time reproduction fees paid for my photographs in the current combined volume of the Ian Allan *ABC of British Railways Locomotives* that had provided the best part of the holiday expenses.

Before being able to obtain my first car in 1958, all these trips had to be taken by train or in a RCTS coach on one of the Society's many area 'shed bashes'. Although most visits centred upon engine sheds, it was usually possible to obtain a few action shots of trains around stations as well, or occasionally from a nearby bridge. The spring-operated shutter on my camera was probably

As a general rule in the 1950s, Gresley 'N2' class 0-6-2Ts worked the local services out of King's Cross and Hill 'N7' class 0-6-2Ts operated similarly from Liverpool Street. However, a small batch of the Hill-designed engines were allocated to Hatfield, and on July 24 1958, one had somehow made its way to King's Cross and was given a heavy haul of empty coaching stock to take from the terminus to Finsbury Park sidings. Class 'N7/5' No. 69632 was the only member of the class I ever photographed on Holloway Bank. Constructed at Gorton Works in January 1926, it was among the last eight 'N7s' to be withdrawn from service in September 1962. One of the eight, No. 69621 was the last engine to be constructed at Stratford Works and was the natural choice for preservation.

It was only upon looking back at my photographic records from the 1950s that I realised just how many different types of film one was obliged to use then. Although the war had been over for some years, film was still difficult to come by and many dealers only stored early supplies of Ilford HP3 or Kodak Super XX under the counter for regular customers. Ilford Selochrome could usually be obtained, but this registered anything red such as the buffer beam as black, and also recorded green foliage as much too dark. Kodak Panatomic X was also obtainable, but excellent lighting was needed for a moving train when operating at 25ASA! Gaevert Gevapan and Agfa Isopan ISS also had to be used on occasions but always produced grainy results, probably due to the fact that I didn't know how to develop them properly. A combination of Ilford HP3 and Meritol Metol developer was my favourite combination, although staining from the developer made my fingers appear as if I smoked about 50 cigarettes a day, when in fact it was only 20! A print made from a negative using my favourite film and developer is Gresley Class 'A3' 4-6-2 No. 60063 *Isinglass* emerging from Copenhagen tunnel on April 30 1955, powering a semi-fast working from King's Cross to Peterborough.

never intended by the makers to be used at its highest speed so often, and after a few years, problems began in this respect and also with the film pressure plate, bringing about two reasons for unsharp negatives. An Agfa Isolette II was by then on the market, and the original camera was traded in for the newer one; this had a slower but more accurate top shutter speed of 1/300 second, but proved adequate for all but the fastest trains at lineside, and in addition it had an excellent four-element f3.5 Solinar lens. This camera was augmented with a Thornton Pickard quarter-plate reflex with a nominal 1/1000 second on the shutter and fitted with a very good f4.5 Cooke Aviar lens. Not caring for glass plates, I had it fitted with a 3¼in x 2¼in roll film holder, which gave an equivalent perspective today of an 85mm lens on a 35mm camera, and was in fact an early form of telephoto effect. Some of my best railway photographs were taken when using this camera, but the focal plane shutter was so erratic that I lost nearly half of the photographs which I took due to blur, and it had to be discarded.

For lineside visits it was necessary to obtain an appropriate permit from the individual BR regions in order legally to gain access to the 'wrong' side of the fence. For this small card it was obligatory to literally 'sign one's life away', as the document that had to be signed before a permit would be issued included words which I recall read something like: 'In the event of injury or death of the permit holder while on railway property within the bounds of this permit, no liability shall attach to the British Railways Board or any of its servants whether or not due to their negligence.' The Southern Region was happy to allow one to photograph anywhere on its non-electrified lines, the

Unbroken sunshine was predicted for Saturday July 5 1952, and a day out on lineside was planned with colleagues Arthur Carpenter and Roy Wilson. Recent lineside permits had been granted to us for a stretch of the Great Central/Great Western Joint Line, and a train from Marylebone took us out to Seer Green for a successful day's photography. Upon arriving back at Marylebone, the 6.15pm 'Master Cutler' express had still to leave. My two friends were required to make their respective ways homeward, but I rather fancied a photograph of the train leaving, particularly since it could not be photographed in the station as it was too long for the platform and the engine was in shadow under the road bridge spanning the terminus. A brisk walk out from the station turned out to be not quite brisk enough, as I just failed to arrive at a position where a shadow would not fall on the engine before it passed me. However, Class 'A3' 4-6-2 No. 60052 *Prince Palatine* still looked good.

Eastern and London Midland Regions were quite content to allow access for many miles of their tracks, but excluding tunnels and viaducts, and the wonderful North Eastern Region and Scottish Region issued permits for their complete territories; after a long paper battle, the Western Region eventually allowed me to join Maurice Earley in the few yards between Twyford and Sonning Cutting!

By now I had successfully applied for membership to the Railway Photographic Society, where prints were entered in circulating portfolios for the other members to comment on, and occasional photo sessions were organised by Lewis Coles at various London engine sheds such as Stewarts Lane and Camden Town. The resultant comments upon my photographs by the likes of Bill Anderson, John Ashman, Eric Bruton, Lewis Coles, Jack Flemons, Cyril Herbert, Pat Ransome-Wallis, Eric Treacy, Pat Whitehouse and Maurice himself, soon brought about a realisation that there was a lot more to the art than I had realised, and drastic improvements in my technique, ideas and composition were brought about that have proved invaluable to this day.

As the decade of the 1950s came to a close, I had some 6,000 negatives of railway subjects, and with assistance from the scraplines at Crewe, Doncaster, Eastleigh and Swindon, had completed my ambition of photographing every type

My first photograph taken with my first 'proper' camera was at Liverpool Street during a lunch hour on March 16 1951. For reasons forgotten in the mists of time my next outing with the camera I have recorded as eight days later at Paddington on March 24. My second recorded negative is a slightly underexposed one of a 'Star' departing from the Great Western terminus, and the third one is this print of platforms 9 and 10 with 'Castle' class 4-6-0 No. 4096 *Highclere Castle* at the buffer-stops, having hauled in empty coaching stock from Old Oak Common to form a train for Bristol Temple Meads, and 'King' class 4-6-0 No. 6005 *King George II* arriving with the 7.30am express from Shrewsbury.

Station lighting at London termini is very good, but this was not always the case. Today, night photography at the likes of Waterloo, King's Cross or Euston, can usually be achieved with an exposure on 400ASA film of a few seconds, using a lens aperture of about f4, in order to record all the necessary detail of a train. In the 1950s, however, there were only light bulbs up in the roof for illumination and exposures were calculated in minutes rather than seconds. A session of night photography around the London stations on January 11 1952, included a few frames spent at St Pancras, where the 8.10pm train for Derby (Midland) was headed by 'Jubilee' class 4-6-0 No. 45651 *Shovell*. This station, with its high domed roof was particularly dim in these days and the exposure needed on the camera for this result is recorded in my ledger as 3 minutes at f8 on 200ASA film. The smallish lens aperture was chosen to avoid passenger movements on the platform being recorded as a blur. The use of f8 meant that providing a person did not stay in one place for more than a few seconds, their image would not appear strongly on the film.

of BR locomotive; the final example was an ex-Caledonian '431' class 2P 0-4-4T banker with cast-iron buffer beam, photographed at Larkfield sidings, near Polmadie, Glasgow. Dieselisation had begun, and while I was quite happy to photograph the early examples, it was with some sadness that I read in the magazines of the ever-increasing number of steam engine withdrawals, some of which had the ominous asterisk against their number, denoting 'last of class'.

With a Rollieflex and then a Zenza Bronica, my cameras were getting better and better, but lineside activities became less and less, and throughout the 1960s I did very little other than go out to record the occasional important-sounding steam rail tour. Following the collapse of a number of motor insurance companies for whom I was by this time acting as a claims assessor, I decided to make a major change in my life, and with an interest in the then new sport of tenpin bowling, switched my occupation from insurance to the leisure industry. After some ten years, a visit to north Wales naturally brought me into contact with the 'Great Little Trains' of that part of the UK, and soon after this an interest in the current BR scene was renewed with a vengeance. Over 20 years on, I am still trying to make up photographically for the missing years, but can never really succeed as I not only missed out on the years of transition to modern traction, but also failed to record the batch of awful diesels that came and went very quickly during the 'dieselisation at all costs' madness of the 1960s.

Many locations which I visited during the 1950s are gone forever, but many others exist, and I still enjoy discovering a pictorial location on a stretch of line not visited before, and recording in a fraction of a second that moment of passing. Whether the train be a preserved steam-hauled special or a 'Eurostar' destined to burrow under the Channel to Europe no longer matters, both are now part of today's railways, and both are equally remote from the days of the 1950s.

While working in the City of London, my station for commuting to and from Kent was Cannon Street. In those days, Sir John Hawkshaw's great crescent roof was still in situ supported by the famous 120ft twin baroque towers. The climate of preservation today probably would not have permitted the roof to be demolished, but this took place as part of a station 'refurbishment' in 1958-9 when it was stated by the 'powers that be' that the roof was in a dangerous condition as a result of age, corrosion and wartime bomb damage. Just the walls, previously supporting the roof, and the towers remained until an office development above the platforms was constructed in the 1990s. This was not particularly sympathetic with the towers, but at least looked better than just the towers themselves stretching somewhat incongruously up into the sky. With the roof still in place, 'L1' class 4-4-0 No. 31787 awaits departure on October 7 1951, with the 12.05pm Sunday train to Charing Cross.

Chris Gammell

The whole country just oozed with steam. When the railways were nationalised in 1948 there were 20,000 steam engines of 400 classes shuffling up and down the system. During the early years of British Railways, from 1951 onwards, 'Standard' classes were introduced and these appeared in every region. The last 'Standard' class of locomotive, 9F 2-10-0 No. 92220 *Evening Star* appeared in 1960 but withdrawals were so rapid that after that date steam had only eight years to run. The 20 years from 1948 until 1968 were certainly glorious in retrospect but were taken for granted at the time. Both the younger and older generations could see the railway in use as the prime mover of the country's people and freight. On the West Coast Main Line fitted freights rattled along the four-track sections every ten minutes during the night while by day sleek 'Pacifics' hauled the express passenger trains. Stanier 'Pacifics', 'Jubilees' and 'Scots' worked the more glamorously named trains and those maids of all work, the LMS 'Black Fives', worked stopping passenger, freight and even the occasional engineers' train. On the East Coast Main Line, Gresley 4-6-2s whisked away the fastest of steam-hauled trains. In the Eastern Region timetable, express trains rushed northward every ten minutes and summer Saturdays spent by the lineside were a pleasing experience. 'Britannias' worked the Hull trains, 'A1s', 'A2s' and 'A3s' worked the Yorkshire and Scottish trains and 'V2' 2-6-2s just about everything. The engines were named after racehorses, birds of prey and anything that sounded sleek and fast. All one had to do was set up a camera and press the shutter as the things flew past.

The South Western lines out of Waterloo were almost as steamy as the other terminals for electrification only reached out to the suburbs. Bulleid 'Pacifics' always made a great show when starting out with a heavy load, be it from Waterloo, Basingstoke or Salisbury. Commencing with that well-known Bulleid moan of a whistle, the driver then opened the cylinder drain cocks as the train edged slowly forward. As soon as the 'spam can' got under way the firework display would commence. The oil-covered track caused the engines to skid violently and the Bulleids would chuff, chunter then skid, and then repeat the operation, slipping away westwards as great palls of smoke filled the air. Once the train had got away the familiar sound of the three-cylinder motion could

be heard as the 'Pacific' chuntered into the distance. To watch a Gresley engine start out of King's Cross was even more spectacular as they had to face the formidable Holloway bank. The antics of engines leaving King's Cross were a tape recordist's dream!

The nation's freight went by rail – motorways were a thing of the future and the roads just too narrow to take heavy goods. Long-distance freights such as coal trains were worked to the big cities and industrial centres. The Western Region sent Welsh coal to London behind Churchward '28XX' class 2-8-0s, and magnificent old crocks they were too. Some of these venerable old plodders have survived into preservation I am glad to say. The LNER had similar 2-8-0s including the three cylinder 'O2s' and the stately Robinson 'O4s' of the former Great Central. Freight was heavy on the GC main line and the Robinson 2-8-0s rattled along it with loaded coal trains southwards and empties northwards. The empties back to the pits were known as 'Windcutters' or 'Annesley

Ivatt 2-6-0 No. 46513 is seen at Pantydwr on the former Cambrian Railway's Mid-Wales line, on August 10 1962. This remote and scenic line, passing through three counties, was opened on September 19 1864 between Moat Lane Junction and Three Cocks Junction, a distance of 48¼ miles. Freight and passenger traffic was always fairly light and inevitable closure came on December 31 1962. Pantydwr station is now a private house.

Runners'. The West Coast line had tottering 0-8-0s of LNWR design known as 'Super Ds', which were later to be replaced by Stanier '8F' 2-8-0s. Two schools of thought prevailed in the design of locomotives, namely, that of Swindon (Collett and Stanier) and that of Doncaster (Gresley and Bulleid). From the larger long-distance locomotive classes sprang lesser designs, including the British 0-6-0. The 0-6-0 was the most common design and could be found everywhere on the system. The 0-6-0 tender locomotive could be seen or heard at work with short-distance trip workings, shunting and local freights. Many town dwellers were lulled to sleep by the incessant huffing and puffing of an 0-6-0 shunting in a local goods yard or blasting away through the night. The rhythmic beats of the exhaust of the local goods plodding away could be heard all over the country. Frequently, a shower of sparks accompanied the exhaust steam as it cut through the night air to make an impressive firework display, with the engine's headlamps glimmering from the front bufferbeam.

I was very fortunate and well advised from the start, as the older generation were only too keen to impart their knowledge and experiences to the younger members of the fraternity. One just had to be a good listener to hear first-hand tales of life before 1923. I was well briefed on what to do and not to do when aiming a camera at trains. There was a great deal of debate at the time as to what type of equipment should be used. Again there were two schools of thought. First, that of the late Maurice Earley who said that all miniature cameras were rubbish and that only large plate cameras should be used. These gave a large surface area on the glass plate and, as a result, gave much better definition. Well, that was quite right, but due to this ball and chain, poor old

A Taunton-Castle Cary stopping train hauled by 0-6-0PT No. 3787 pauses at Charlton Mackrell station in July 1962. This section of line was opened in 1906 as part of the GWR 'cut-off' that shortened the distance between Paddington and the West of England. Few people used the intermediate stations and the local passenger service was sparse, being withdrawn on September 10 1962 shortly after this photograph was taken. The complete GWR station of 1906 can be seen here, attractively surrounded by Scots pine trees, shrubs and plants; the wooden lower-quadrant starting signal completes the scene.

Maurice never got much beyond Sonning Cutting. Secondly, the miniature camera school had a lightweight piece of equipment which could be taken anywhere. The debate raged for years with the large format brigade refusing to accept the more modern methods.

The choice of colour film was another source of endless debate as the Kodak-ites battled it out with the Agfa-ites. Agfa was a much faster film but was not so fine-grained as the slower Kodak film. When slides were projected onto a screen at the local railway club the Kodak-ites would jeer at the Agfa film as being too coarse and grainy. The Agfa-ites would consider that the Kodak film was too slow and that only the best of lighting conditions would provide good results. The dreadful British climate did not help the case of Kodak film but the Kodak-ites eventually won, as the Agfa film tended to fade with time. Somebody brought a consumer report to a club meeting and read it out to the assembled crowd. The report stated that as far as could be ascertained, Kodak colour slides would last for ever if properly stored. A lot of railway enthusiasts keep their films in the living room where central heating and gas fires in particular are bad news for film storage. Always store your films in a cool dry place and take them out now and again to see what state they are in. Fungus can grow on the emulsion and this is very difficult to remove.

With a good camera and the right film I was able to tramp around the countryside at will. I had a Baldalux camera with a lovely Schneider lens which gave sharp pictures, but the shutter speeds were a little on the slow side. With a slow shutter speed and a fine aperture, sharp results could be obtained. Another piece of luck for me was that I worked for British Railways from an early age and was able to travel all over the place at a very cheap rate, which was based on 1947 fares. When a new entrant had completed one year's service

Dudbridge, on the former Midland Railway branch to Nailsworth and Stroud (Midland), sees LMS '4F' 0-6-0 No. 44264 shunting the daily goods in 1963. The branches to Nailsworth and Stroud were closed to passengers on June 8 1949, but goods traffic lingered on until June 1 1966. Dudbridge station building is now a private house. A total of 575 engines of the '4F' class 0-6-0s were built by the LMS between 1924 and 1941, No. 44264 being built in 1926.

BR Standard Class '5' 4-6-0 No. 73090, based at Shrewsbury, heads northwards near Pontardulais on the Central Wales line on June 15 1963 with a Swansea Victoria-Shrewsbury through train. There were five trains each weekday over the 115¼ miles, which included a through Swansea-York working. Swansea Victoria (the ex-LNWR station) to Pontardulais closed to all traffic on June 15 1964, but the rest of the Central Wales line is still open. The section of line from Pontardulais to Llandilo was part of he former GWR system and the line from Llandilo to Llandovery was jointly owned by the GWR and the LNWR. North of Llandovery the line was owned by the LNWR, later to become part of the LMS system.

Opposite The platforms at Morebath were extended by the GWR to cater for increased train lengths as traffic developed on the picturesque Taunton-Barnstaple line. GWR 2-6-0 No. 7304 is seen here on the Taunton-Barnstaple train on July 9 1962. The 44¾-mile branch to Barnstaple was opened by the Bristol & Exeter Railway in 1873 as a broad gauge line and became part of the GWR system in 1876, before being converted to standard gauge in 1881. Passenger services at the remotely situated stations were withdrawn on October 3 1966.

on the railways he was entitled to use free tickets. There was an annual all-BR ticket and three regional ones with an increased quota as time went by. The travel opportunities were endless (I once went to Teheran on a free ticket!) and you don't have to make a career out of it. Just do a few years and then move on. Too many of my friends who had ambitious parents were forced into accountancy, banking and the professions, which they did not really like, and have subsequently led thoroughly miserable lives. It was a wonderful way to spend one's teens, endless travel for next to nothing!

The late W. A. Camwell, known universally as 'Cam', organised many rail tours around the Midlands and Wales during the 1950s and 1960s. Some of the tours were classics and we went on several specials around the Welsh Valleys. The usual method of travel was by the 1am Paddington to Swansea which stopped at Reading, Swindon, Gloucester, Chepstow, Newport and Cardiff. The 5.37am arrival at Cardiff was convenient for a 'Cam' special in the Valleys. Many memorable specials were run, including the last train from Abergavenny to Merthyr on January 5 1958 behind an LNWR 0-8-0 No. 49121 and the last coal tank No. 58926 (now preserved). The former LNWR line crossed the heads of the valleys and connected with the valley lines at the top end. This spectacular railway had severe gradients and started with a 1-in-34 climb for ¾-mile to Govilon and continued on for another two miles at 1-in-

Ex-GWR 0-6-0PT No. 4662 stops with a loose-coupled freight on the Penygraig branch in Glamorgan on July 2 1960. The train has stopped to enable the guard to pin down the wagon brakes as the gradient is severe. Some of the Welsh valley lines had gradients as steep as 1-in-38 and 'Stop Boards' were provided with instructions that all loose-coupled freight trains should comply with the regulations relating to pinning-down brakes. The engine is painted in the British Railways unlined black livery of the 1948-1956 period with the lion and wheel crest on the tank sides. Passenger services on the Penygraig branch were withdrawn on June 9 1958 and freight on April 3 1967.

'57XX' class 0-6-0PT No. 7736 leaves Dowlais Top station with the 2.05pm Brecon-Newport stopping passenger train on February 24 1962. The scenic Brecon & Merthyr line included the four miles at 1-in-38 to Torpantau summit and the 1-in-40 from Darran & Deri. The line closed to passengers on December 31 1962. Part of the trackbed is now occupied by the narrow-gauge Brecon Mountain Railway which operates from Pant, not far from the location of this photograph. The BMR is gradually extending its operation through Torpantau tunnel to a new terminus.

38 to Clydach. The former LNWR built special engines for the line in the form of powerful 0-8-4 side tanks. After the last train had run, most of the trackbed was converted into a road. A similar scenic ride could be enjoyed on the Brecon & Merthyr which included the climb to Torpantau summit from Pentir Rhiw through thick forest. The gradient from Pentir Rhiw to the summit was at 1-in-38 for the four miles. The summit was at 1,313ft and the view spectacular, for the railway could be seen winding its way up the hills. Part of the trackbed is now occupied by the narrow-gauge Brecon Mountain Railway.

The Mid-Wales line was another scenic piece of railway and ran from the Cambrian main line at Moat Lane Junction to Talyllyn Junction, a distance of 56 miles. The railway ran through three counties and traversed some fine countryside. This former Cambrian backwater was opened in 1864 and became part of the GWR system as a result of the grouping. The line was scheduled to close on December 31 1962, so a visit in the summer of that year was just in time. I visited all the stations on the line and had a ride on a freight to Boughrood where the signalman was standing in his box having a shave. He had just put the shaving soap on his face when I arrived and told him that I wanted a ticket. I asked him to open up the booking office as the train was due. The signalman picked up his keys and rushed off to the office to open up, forgetting all about his shaving. Having purchased the ticket I boarded the train with the guard, loco crew and all of the passengers roaring with laughter as the signalman could be seen on the platform still with shaving cream adorning his face.

In the same week I visited the Kington branch, which was worked by a '14XX' class 0-4-2T from Leominster. The train left at 8.45am and ran on weekdays only. On Tuesdays and Thursdays the train worked to Presteigne over a line which had closed to passengers in 1951. A ride on a Collett '14XX' was great fun, and on this occasion I had No. 1447, with an informative crew who told me that they had invented a new method of ordering their lunch. When the train approached Kington on the return from Presteigne the fireman would give a few blasts on the whistle – one for cod and two for chips. When the engine crew got round to the fish and chip shop the order would be waiting on the counter, ready salted and vinegared. The Welsh Valleys teemed with steam during this period and the traffic was heavy. The section from Bassaleg to Park Junction near Newport, known to railwaymen as the 'Golden Mile', was of six tracks such was the density of traffic. The engine allocations at the sheds in the area reflected the importance of the traffic. Ebbw Junction had 141 engines on the books during the early 1950s and heavy freight types such as the '42XX' class 2-8-0T and the '72XX' class 2-8-2Ts as well as the '28XX' 2-8-0s were well represented. BR 'Standard' class 2-10-0s were also used as well as the '56XX' class 0-6-2 tanks. The '57XX' class panniers could be seen all over the place and were a vast class of over 800 engines ideal for local trip work and shunting. Several of the ex-GWR '57XX' class panniers have survived as some were sold secondhand to London Transport and lasted well after steam had finished on BR. 'The Glorious Years' finished all too soon but there was plenty of steam left in other countries, so one simply just went abroad. Today, many of the sights and sounds of those years can be seen on Britain's preserved lines where a ride soon brings back memories of the long-lost past.

Another view of pannier tank No. 4662, this time shunting at Clydach Vale colliery, Glamorgan, on July 2 1960 during the pit's annual holiday period. The colliery in Clydach Vale was served by the GWR and Taff Vale Railway, the GWR branch from Penygraig being an extension of the Ely Valley line and opened on August 10 1878. The Taff Vale branch to Clydach Vale opened in 1889 and was an extension of the Pwllyrhebog branch opened in 1863. The TVR branch had a gradient of 1-in-13 which was cable-operated, utilising the 'H' class 0-6-0T humpback engines built by Kitsons. The TVR branch was closed on July 1 1951 and the 'H' class locomotives withdrawn soon after.

Paul Riley

Born 1945
Died August 22 1976

An appreciation by Ian Krause
Captions by Derek Huntriss

Opposite 'Jubilee' 4-6-0 No. 45605 *Cyprus* leaves Gloucester Eastgate and passes under the unique Barton Street Junction signalbox with a Bristol bound express in July 1963. Generally speaking the Midland was a line with small neat signalboxes made of wood throughout and painted yellow. The average Midland box had quite a short lever frame, partly because facing points and facing point locks were worked by the same lever and partly because the Midland was relatively sparing in the provision of shunting signals. Indeed, the largest Midland Railway box, at St Pancras Junction, had only 132 levers. The box floors were generally covered in linoleum and the lighting at night kept dim, the idea being to help the signalman to see the engine numbers by the aid of a large lamp fixed outside the box on the front.

The three-day-old Ford Escort's speedo had just notched the 'ton' when it hit the first of the three humps on the road from Ingleton to Ribblehead. A few seconds, a hundred yards of dry stone wall and four wheels hurtling in different directions later, the once-new car was on its back, its engine on fire. Two of the occupants were lying, semi-conscious, in a ditch filled with stinging nettles at the side of the road. The driver, Paul Riley, a little dazed and confused, staggered the half mile to the Hill Inn – not for help, but to join in the Ribblehead Reunion celebrations. It was, after all, August the Eleventh, 1975.

Three weeks in the Airedale General Hospital, a John Poulson building that hasn't yet fallen down, gave me plenty of scope to reflect on the man who had just attempted to kill myself and his girlfriend. The doctor had professed his wonderment that anyone could have survived a crash that, quite literally, left an unrecognisable lump of metal in place of the pride of the Coventry hire-car fleet. A year later, almost to the day, Paul Riley was dead.

As a wide-eyed, but not yet legless photographer in the 1960s, I had my heroes. W. J. V. Anderson was the first – head and shoulders above Maurice Earley, Eric Treacy and the like. Then there was Colin Gifford, the first, and probably only, railway photographer who could relate steam to its social environment. And then there was Paul Riley.

The Waverley Route was the most under-photographed of lines; Bill Anderson barely touched it, Eric Treacy stuck to the accessible bits. But, around 1964, pictures started appearing in *Trains Illustrated* that opened up the wonders of that most remote region of Britain. Steele Road and Riccarton Junction began to replace the Beattocks and Shaps in my imagination. Almost exclusively, the captions were credited to one 'P. Riley'.

A classic shot depicting Carlisle Kingmoor (12A) MPD's well-groomed 'Britannia' 4-6-2 No. 70045 *Lord Rowallan* as it nears Shap station with a Carlisle-Manchester Red Bank parcels in December 1967. Monday January 1 1968 was the date which announced the opening of a new diesel depot simply known as Carlisle. In turn, this meant the complete closure of Carlisle Kingmoor MPD and brought to an end the regular use of steam traction over Shap and the Settle & Carlisle routes. *Lord Rowallan's* final duty was to haul the 1.10pm Carlisle-Skipton goods on December 30 1967, the last steam-hauled train to leave Carlisle before Kingmoor depot was closed.

I had a vision of 'P. Riley'. I'd met R. C. Riley, a charming man who wore a suit and worked in the City. P. Riley's pictures, on the whole, were not very different from those of his namesake. So, should I ever chance to meet him, I expected an urbane, middle-aged man of impeccable style and manners.

Leeds City Station, August 1967. I was on my way to Holbeck with a friend when we happened to wander into a seedy little café in Jack Lane. And there, huddled under a dingy 40-watt light, mouth full of over-cooked baked beans and bacon with the rind still on, sat the object of my adulation. I suddenly realised that I knew him. We'd met and exchanged pleasantries the year before.

Blue Peter had been heading for Aberdeen from Edinburgh – the last time it would work a real train between those cities. It was a Saturday in late August. My car load had positioned themselves on Dalgety bank, just east of Inverkeithing. The train was due in three minutes. Suddenly, a car screeched to a halt, four bodies hurtled down the embankment and up trees and telegraph poles. It was only then that they realised we were blocking their shots. Amidst the torrent of abuse that rang round the cutting, I gathered they'd cleaned the engine. It arrived in mid-torrent; the driver's response to their efforts was to open the cylinder cocks and render the shot almost useless. The Midland Neverers Association had unwittingly arrived in my life.

Nine months later, the self-same picture landed on my doorstep. Mike Higson, then owner of the late-lamented Roundhouse bookshop in Harrow, had asked me to help him try and compile a definitive *Steam in Scotland* photographic album. W. J. V. Anderson had finally been persuaded, Derek Cross was no problem. But there was no decent coverage of the Waverley Route. So I wrote to P. Riley. Back came a courteous letter and some 15in x 12in prints of such dire quality that we couldn't use them, including No. 60532 at Dalgety. Fast forward to Jack Lane, Leeds.

Six in the morning had rendered Paul fairly harmless, so we got chatting. He didn't do his own printing. As far as he was concerned, the taking of the picture was almost more important than the end result. It was an attitude that was to change quite rapidly, as did his approach to photography. The entourage sitting around him in the café's squalor were all names that I recognised from the railway press – C. E. Weston, D. Gouldthorp, M. York, P. Claxton. They were fairly uncommunicative; some still are. But they obviously looked up to Paul as the unspoken leader of their ad hoc group. By the end of breakfast, he and I had agreed to disagree on our views of photography, but became friends until his death.

The official line on Paul Riley is that he pioneered the use of the telephoto lens in railway photography, but, let's try a different tack. His photography can be split into three separate periods –1961-5 and 1966-8 as far as his black and white work is concerned, and, as a separate study, the pictures he produced in colour. Let's begin at the beginning.

The 'photographic' elite of the post-war years were, by and large, fairly well-off users of large format or 6x6 cameras. There were exceptions – R. E Vincent and C. C. B. Herbert were both avid enthusiasts for 35mm. But we're talking Leicas here, not Halina 35xs or the like. Paul Riley was young, fairly impoverished, and wanted to emulate W. J. V. Anderson. So, instead of a Zeiss Ikonta or the vastly more expensive Linhof Technica that both Anderson and Cross were using, he settled for a humble Pentax 35mm. His early work around the Midlands and places like Stoke Bank on the East Coast main line is still interesting rather than exceptional – good quality, straight-down-the-middle, front three-quarter views of main line steam. His published work in 1963-4 was very much in the mould

Some of the famous Gresley 'A4' class 'Pacifics' performed their final duties, rather ironically, on the 'three-hour' expresses of the former LMS main line between Glasgow and Aberdeen. They were kept in splendid condition as can be seen in this view of No. 60024 *Kingfisher*, seen leaving Gleneagles in the summer of 1966 with the 1.30pm Aberdeen-Glasgow train.

The spectacle we have traded for the understated, super-efficient electrics: a Stanier Class '5' blasts towards Scout Green in December 1967, assisted by one of Tebay MPD's Riddles BR 4-6-0s. Some two years earlier the banking duties had been entrusted to Fairburn 2-6-4Ts.

of Bill Anderson – dramatic, low-angle, slightly condensed in perspective. Anderson always used a slightly longer than normal focal-length lens on his plate cameras, and, in about 1965, Paul Riley discovered the telephoto lens. It was a discovery that was to change the face of conventional railway photography.

Whether Paul Riley 'invented' the use of the telephoto lens or not is debatable; what is certain is that he produced some of the greatest and most powerful images ever to leave the back of a camera. Perhaps it was something to do with his character, but the images he produced were about the masculinity of the steam engine – forget any thoughts about calling a 'Duchess' a 'she'; Riley's pictures, like his lifestyle, left little to the imagination. That is not a criticism. The vast majority of well-published railway photographers have seen their work in print thanks to the quality of their camera lenses rather than the quality of their perception. Paul Riley was different.

In the days before motor-drives, he would happily run off three rolls of Agfa CT18 before breakfast. Invariably, this scatter-gun approach paid off: he had a love of the landscape that could make virtually every frame a 'master shot' – witness his coverage of No. 70013 working the last passenger train up Shap on Boxing Day, 1967, the superb sequence of No. 48448 battling up to Copy Pit early in 1968, or his footage on Shap in December 1967 of backlit freights taken on a 400mm lens which cost a fraction of a filter for a Linhof. They are the work of a master. Sadly, though, a vast quantity of Paul Riley's work has bypassed an entire generation.

Black and white was the real name of the game as far as Paul was concerned. His Waverley Route shots, as already mentioned, have not been surpassed. In 1967, he took what is arguably the greatest image of a train in action in this country that has ever graced the pages of a magazine. 'Jubilee' class 4-6-0 No.

A splendid night shot depicting 'Jubilee' No. 45675 *Hardy* inside York (50A) MPD after cleaning by the MNA enthusiast group in December 1966. The 'Jubilee' had finished her summer excursion duties from Holbeck (55A) MPD and was on loan to York for passing out firemen. Having lost the last 3-cylinder loco from York, 'V2' No. 60831, in December 1966, the foreman insisted that firemen were passed out on both 2-cylinder and 3-cylinder locos, hence the need for the 'Jubilee' 4-6-0.

45562 *Alberta* was working a rail tour north from the West Riding to Carlisle on an autumn Saturday. The weather was just right, good three-quarter back lighting on Dillicar Troughs, half a mile out of Tebay. Paul and some friends jammed the troughs open. A 135mm lens and full sun conjured up an image that has graced countless book covers and periodicals. There was even a 60in x 40in framed print in the Junction Hotel in Tebay throughout the 1970s and early 1980s. But the hotel changed name and hands, and the print went missing. The hotel is now retirement flats, and the print is still missing. But more worryingly, so is the original negative.

What is arguably one of the most exciting photographic collections in the British Isles remains shrouded in secrecy. The MNA, an acronym for the Midland Neverers Association, was an organisation founded on a common desire to travel by train while avoiding paying for the privilege. Its members also cleaned engines in their spare time. Paul Riley was the unspoken and unopposed leader. There was a feeling of almost Masonic brotherhood about the organisation when it flourished in the mid-1960s. Sadly, not a lot has changed, and Paul Riley's contribution to the development of black and white photography remains locked up in somebody's misguided vision of keeping the old memories pure. Riley's remarkable vision deserves a better epitaph.

So enjoy what you see here, and search back into the 1960s world of *Trains Illustrated* and *Modern Railways*. If you want to read about Paul in his own words, hunt for back copies of *Steam Railway* for June and July 1992. His eloquent descriptions of travels by bike, RDU 290, and 'Britannias' is as good a way as any into the mind of somebody who could climb up the outside of the Castle Keep in Newcastle in order to get the master shot without paying, could climb an electricity pylon to see off a 'Q6', or dive off Cleethorpes Pier while the tide was out, thereby breaking both wrists and rendering himself unemployable as a roadie for a folk band.

Paul Riley did not ignore the more traditional approach and produced some fine lineside three-quarter views. Here GWR Class '41XX' 2-6-2T No. 4100 heads a rake of BR Mark 1 stock away from Gloucester Central towards Tramway Junction. Transferred to Gloucester Horton Road (85B) MPD from Kidderminster (85D) in July 1957 No. 4100 continued in traffic at Gloucester until withdrawn at the end of Western Region steam in November 1965. After one month in store at 85B No. 4100 was taken to Buttigiegs scrap yard in Newport where she was broken up in February 1966.

Stanier '8F' 2-8-0 No. 48442 heads a Gowhole Yard-Buxton freight near Chinley on February 3 1968. The previous night had seen frantic activity at Buxton MPD as members of the MNA enthusiast group returned No. 48442 to immaculate condition. Attempts to photograph her outward trip had been thwarted by early morning fog and uncleaned sister '8F' No. 48327 headed the first train to appear in good light. This section of the former Midland Railway route near Chinley was widened to accommodate four tracks in 1902 and the tunnel which had previously existed at Buxworth was demolished and replaced by a deep cutting. Present-day improvements in motive power and reductions in traffic have once again seen the return to a straightforward double-track layout, the two lines farthest from the camera having been removed.

Opposite Careful use of a 135mm telephoto lens emphasises the struggle of man and machine climbing towards Ais Gill summit. With the snow covered slopes of Wild Boar Fell as a backdrop, Stanier Class '5' 4-6-0 No. 44912 slogs up the last few yards of 1-in-100 gradient with an up freight in April 1967.

People have called Paul Riley an enigma. He wasn't. His mission was to enjoy life to the full. The sports jacket and suit brigade of the railway fraternity could never quite cope with him. My last memory of him, other than the near-miss in 1975, was the arrival of H. M. Constabulary at a respectable house in Sandbanks, Dorset, in 1974. Who, they enquired, was the owner of the potato lorry from Coventry which was parked outside? 'Well, officer, I only borrowed it for the weekend.' One afternoon in August 1976, whilst in search of yet another 'master shot', Paul had fallen asleep on the parapet of Victoria Bridge, Severn Valley Railway. In his slumber he rolled off the bridge, falling sixty feet to his death. You can run as many special freight trains for photographers as you like, but you'll never re-create Paul Riley.

Geoff Rixon

It seems many moons ago now that, as a young lad in the late 1930s, I became interested in railways. I was the proud owner of an '0' gauge Hornby 'Royal Scot' railway set, and was collecting my Dad's Wills cigarette cards. In 1943 I acquired my first Ian Allan *ABCs*: the Southern Railway *ABC*, and the London Midland & Scottish Railway *ABC,* both costing about a shilling – I had the bug.

My school was a stone's throw from the Southern main line at Hampton Court Junction and the best view was from the biology room on the first floor. I may not have learnt much about plants and animals, but I certainly made a few 'cops', including the Bulleid 'Merchant Navy' class (nicknamed 'flannel jackets'), which were taking over from the 'Lord Nelsons' and 'King Arthurs'.

I wanted to spot some of the big LMS streamlined locomotives that I had seen in my *ABC*. With instructions from Dad I set out to reach Willesden Junction; care was needed when travelling in the war years. I took a bus to Richmond station, where I picked up one of the old London & North Western Railway electrics on the North London line. These quaint machines had sliding doors at the end of each coach, with the company insignia engraved in the glass.

On reaching Willesden overhead station I asked the ticket collector where I could find the main line. A large, old wooden staircase, leading down to the main line platform, confronted me. I heard a heavy beat, but didn't know quite which way to look. A 'streak' was approaching – I couldn't believe my luck: No. 6237 *City of Bristol* still in its pre-war livery of red with gold stripes. These were the only two 'Coronations' still in their pre-war livery, and it was especially nice to see a splash of colour at a time when most locomotives were looking drab in their wartime colours. These junction visits became a Saturday ritual, especially as there was the added attraction of two massive locomotive sheds – Willesden 1A and Old Oak Common 81A – just down the road.

During the war the unexpected became the ordinary. On one visit I was on the station platform when the air raid siren sounded. The next minute, clutching my *ABC*, I found myself watching RAF fighter planes battling German bombers.

By 1947 I was working as an apprentice cabinet maker. My pay packet yielded just over two pounds a week, but I was keen to try my hand at

photography and I set my sights on the Brownie box camera which my Dad obtained by collecting Kellog's cereal coupons. He agreed to let me use it, but getting the 116 SRE film was a problem until a friend found a few rolls of ex-RAF reconnaissance film in Petticoat Lane market.

My very first shot, taken at Euston in April 1947, was of 'Royal Scot' No. 6121. With tremendous care I held the camera at waist height, took a deep breath and clicked, hoping it hadn't moved. Apart from a few streaks of light the results were quite remarkable – much sharper than I had expected for the camera and film.

Sensing adventure was to be found further afield, I met up with a friend to take an economy trip northbound. We were both very enthusiastic, but had little cash – just a pocket full of shed permits. We headed out of Euston on the 'Irish Mail', hauled by a double-headed loco combination of a Holyhead rebuilt 'Royal Scot', being piloted by a Crewe North 'Jubilee'. It was an exhilarating run to Crewe, where we alighted at some unearthly hour on a Saturday morning. After an hour exploring this very busy station it was time to catch a couple of hours' sleep. That was wishful thinking, as an early arrival Football Special came in with its team supporters chanting and waving their rattles. It was then time to continue our tour further north to Liverpool and Manchester, with permits for such sheds as Bank Hall, Edge Hill, Aintree and Longsight. Things went to plan, with the exception of the sleeping arrangements for which no provision had been made. However, a night spent in the cosy waiting room at Liverpool Exchange Station, with its long padded bench seats, was fine, until the long arm of the law woke us up with a shake at 3am. We had to explain why we were there, but the remaining shed permits spread on the table worked a miracle, and we were allowed to stay. The next night, at Manchester Central,

'Coronation' class 4-6-2 No. 46238 *City of Carlisle* is shown being turned on the giant Camden 1B loco shed turntable, after working into Euston with an express from Stranraer on August 4 1962. Camden loco shed was situated one-and-a-half miles north of Euston at the summit of a 1-in-77 climb, and finally closed for steam traffic on September 9 1963. No. 46238, whose home shed since 1948 was 12B Carlisle Upperby, was in its usual immaculate condition. The crimson livery with LMS-style lining was applied between December 1957 and November 1958, and was also carried by 14 other members of the class. Starting out in life in September 1938 as one of the LMS streamlined 'Pacifics', No. 46238 was de-streamlined in November 1946 and was finally withdrawn from service in September 1964.

REFRESHMENT FACILITIES

GREAT HALL · CAFETERIA & BUFFET

PLATFORM 13 · BUFFET

46208

'Princess Royal' class 'Pacific' No. 46208 *Princess Helena Victoria*, shedded at 8A Edge Hill (Liverpool), is seen on arrival at Euston from Liverpool in June 1953. The loco is sporting the BR Brunswick green livery and in 1958 was one of four members of the class which received a crimson livery. No. 46208 was one of the regulars on the Liverpool run, being at the 8A shed for the last 11 years of its 27-year life, from August 1951 until withdrawn from service in September 1962. I must say that the arrival end of Euston station was one of my favourite London termini locations for photography with its old LNWR herringbone roof structure and open-ended platforms without ticket barriers.

a similar thing happened, only this time we were not so lucky, being escorted at dawn on to our return train to London, with a few films used and our note books bulging with numbers. This, our very first tour, would be the one to remember forever.

In 1950 I had to serve two years National Service with the Royal Artillery. This halted my railway activity as I was posted to Cyprus, where the railway had just shut down. Demob came in 1952. Feeling quite flush with my army pay of £30, I made for the camera shop to purchase my very first new camera, an Ensign Selfix 820, with an eight-speed f3.8 lens, using 120 film. The lens was extremely good, but with the shutter speed being 1/250 second, getting the timing and angle exactly right was essential if I was to eliminate the front number blur on moving trains.

This camera gave me the confidence to obtain the shots I had always hoped for. The next step was to reach other locations around the country. In 1954, earning a little more money, I managed to get some wheels – a Lambretta scooter (on hire purchase, of course). These economical scooters were all the rage in the mid-1950s – the only drawback was that they exposed you to the elements. I was raring to go, and one summer Saturday I set off for Exeter.

The congestion caused by holiday traffic meant that the whole journey was spent crawling down the middle of the road, but it was all worth it, since once I reached Exeter St David's station I had quite a mind-boggling experience, with tightly packed trains arriving every few minutes from every corner of the country. In those days, there were many double-headed locomotive combinations; for instance, it was quite common to see a 'Grange' or 'Hall' class being piloted by a BR Standard Class '9F' 2-10-0. On that busy Saturday I used up seven rolls of film – 84 shots.

A couple of years later, in 1956, I visited the West Country again to photograph the Cornish branch line from Bere Alston to Callington, and the inevitable happened: I met a young lady living in a cottage at the Callington terminus (it wasn't every day that the village saw a leather-coated chap drive in on a flash scooter). We got on like a house on fire and, as an added bonus, her uncle who lived with her was the Callington line's senior driver. About a year later this lady moved up to Surrey, and in 1960 she married me. I was very lucky to find a wife who shared my hobby.

In 1959, on a visit to Scotland, I tried out my first colour slide film – 10ASA Kodachrome. In 1960, 25ASA became available, and I bought a new Pentax S2 camera with a 55mm Takumar lens. I was hooked on colour, although there were problems when conditions were unfavourable for this brilliant but slow

A heavy ballast train from Meldon Quarry grinds to a halt in the centre road at Exeter St David's station. The locomotive in charge of the train on July 20 1953 is an 'N' class 'Mogul' No. 31851, based at 72A Exmouth Junction shed. The loco waits with its train for assistance at the rear from a pair of Class 'E/1r' 0-6-0Ts before climbing the steep incline up to Exeter Central station. The Southern Railway 'N' class locos were designed by Maunsell in 1925. Parts for most of the class were made at the military establishment at Woolwich Arsenal. Boilers were constructed by North British Locomotive Works and then the Southern Locomotive works at Ashford carried out the final assembly work. No. 31851 had a life span of 38 years before being withdrawn in September 1963.

film. The available options, if you wanted faster film, were Kodak Ektachrome, which seemed very grainy, Gevacolour, which suffered from red overtones, and Agfa, a good hard sharp film but not so natural in colour terms. However, it didn't really matter what type of colour film you used, as the general condition of the locomotives was deteriorating rapidly through lack of cleaning.

I next decided to try to capture the grime and smoke around the locomotive sheds, the atmosphere in the roundhouses, and the men going about their daily tasks of oiling up, watering and coaling their machines. There was so much potential here. This was also true of the stations. Euston was a favourite of mine, with its old herringbone roof, open-ended arrival platforms and old enamel tinplate signs. These kinds of shot are virtually impossible to recreate in preservation.

As the years ticked by you were confronted by lines of withdrawn locomotives at nearly every railway shed or yard. There was a sense of urgency, and you felt it was essential to try to record as much as possible before the whole scene was swept away. Visiting Willesden Junction in July 1967 I could have cried at the sight of the roundhouse and other buildings being flattened. I walked around, taking a few shots, thinking I must have trod every inch of the place over the years. A year later, steam on British Railways came to an end and I put my camera away in disgust.

In the mid-1970s, by which time I had two small sons, I blew the dust off my cameras and started to take them round the preservation scene. In the early 1980s I bought a Canon A1 with a f1.4 lens, and began to feel quite enthusiastic again. But the scene now is certainly very different. Having been a solitary figure at the lineside, I now rub shoulders with many others trying to take the ultimate shot, and who would have thought that one would see traffic jams in desolate Cumbria! Still, I mustn't complain, but count myself lucky to have captured at least some of the steam era on film.

London's Marylebone station, the capital's terminus of the Great Central Railway, sets the scene for this photograph. Visiting the station on the morning of Saturday August 18 1962 was 21A Saltley-based Class '5MT' 4-6-0 No. 44814, simmering at the buffer stops, bathed in sunshine, after working through the night with the up cheap fare 'Starlight Special' from Edinburgh (Waverley). There was a similar service that ran from Glasgow (St Enoch) into St Pancras. The Stanier 'Black 5s' were certainly the most widely used class of locomotives working on main lines in Britain, their performance being second to none. This was surely judged by the fact that no fewer than 842 of the class were built between 1934 and 1951. No. 44814, built at Derby in 1944, completed 23 years of service life before being withdrawn in September 1967.

Above A reminder of the Peppercorn 'A1' class 'Pacifics'. Working on top link traction, No. 60123 *H. A. Ivatt*, of 56C Copley Hill (Leeds) shed, leaves King's Cross station in very clean external condition on Saturday August 19 1962 with the 3.55pm train for Leeds. Just three weeks after this photograph was taken, No. 60123 had transferred to 56D Ardsley (Leeds) shed. Whilst working the 8.50pm goods train from King's Cross to Leeds on September 7 1962 tragedy struck at Offord in Huntingdonshire when the train ran into the rear of the 8.25pm King's Cross-Newcastle Forth goods train. As a result No. 60123 was so badly damaged that it was withdrawn from service on October 1 1962, having had a life span of only 13 years.

Left The crowds gather, lining the platform ends at London's King's Cross station, for this very unusual pairing of locomotive power. The occasion was the Ian Allan special excursion train to Doncaster Works on April 20 1960. The Midland 'Compound' 4-4-0 No. 1000, borrowed for the occasion from the LMR, with its crew from Kentish Town shed, was being piloted by Great Western 4-4-0 No. 3440 *City of Truro*. The outward run to Doncaster was completed satisfactorily but alas on the return trip to London, No. 3440 succumbed to overheating, causing an unscheduled stop at Fletton Junction.

Above 'A3' class 'Pacific' No. 60041 *Salmon Trout*, shedded at 64A St Margaret's (Edinburgh), is seen on London Midland Region metals being turned by her driver on the Carlisle Kingmoor turntable, after working south on a freight train duty. This locomotive, being the last but one of the class to survive in service, was built in 1934 and allocated to 64B Haymarket, where it resided for 26 years until July 1960. It then moved over to St Margaret's for the remainder of its service life until withdrawal on December 4 1965. Its final resting place was the breaker's yard of Arnott & Young of Carmyle in September 1966. The loco still carried an original Great Northern coal-railed tender which was fitted in 1937. Parts of No. 60041 still survive. I believe the boiler was a spare for the preserved No. 60103 *Flying Scotsman* and its double chimney was purchased by a gentleman from Basingstoke, and is on loan to the *Flying Scotsman*, which it carries in its present BR form today.

Opposite top 'Coronation' class 'Pacific' No. 46235 *City of Birmingham* which had been a resident of 5A Crewe North shed since 1948, receives its final preparation on Glasgow's 66A Polmadie shed yard on September 15 1959. With a full head of steam it was due to set off with an express from Glasgow Central for its 400-mile haul to London Euston. This locomotive was built in a streamlined condition by the LMS at Crewe in 1939 and originally decked out in a livery of crimson with gold stripes. However, when built, World War II was imminent and, like most other locomotives, it soon received an all-over black livery. Just after the end of the war in 1945 a decision was taken to de-streamline the class and No. 46235 lost its casing in April 1946. It received the BR Brunswick green livery in the early 1950s and worked in regular service until withdrawal in September 1964. No. 46235 turned out to be one of the lucky survivors of the class, missing the breaker's torch by being preserved in the Birmingham Museum of Science & Industry.

Opposite below This very busy and cluttered looking scene of lines of locomotives undergoing overhaul was taken on Thursday August 20 1953 in the main erecting shop at Crewe Works, on the occasion of a visit arranged by British Railways. On arrival at Crewe, a special train that had started out from Euston and hauled by BR Standard Class '5MT' 4-6-0 No. 73020 was taken right inside the works, where the alighting passengers received an extensive four-hour tour, split into groups, each with its own guide. I was very pleased to obtain several good photographs, showing the atmosphere of life in a loco works, but in achieving this, of course, I had to slip the ranks occasionally.

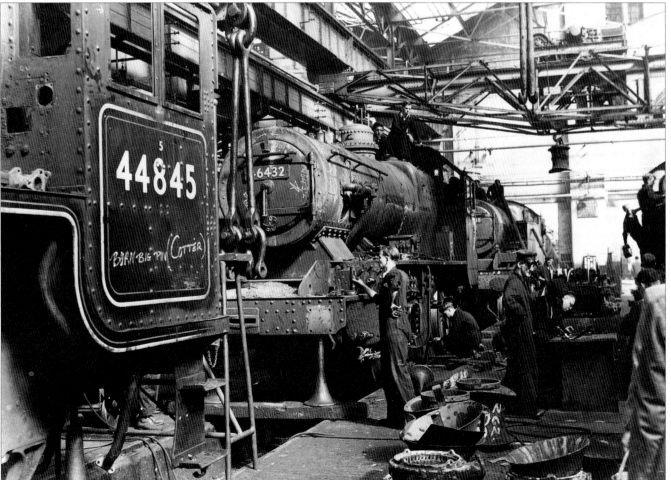

Mike Esau

I suppose the Second World War and the Great Western Railway were responsible for starting my interest in railways. I was two years old when the war started, and as the conflict grew more serious and the bombing of London began, my mother and I went to stay with my father's relatives in Newcastle Emlyn in west Wales. Life was not that easy for my mother marooned so far from home, especially as our relatives often preferred to speak in Welsh rather than English! Probably to keep me amused, my mother used to take me down to the station to see the trains which had arrived from Pencader on the Carmarthen-Aberystwyth line. Since Newcastle Emlyn was at the end of the branch, there was plenty of time to enjoy the trains, which were usually hauled by pannier tanks. It was not long before I was allowed on the footplate, and although I was a little scared the first time, the experience must have made a lasting impression on me, for I can still clearly recall standing in front of the firebox and seeing the huge steam dome through the spectacle glass of the cab. I think it is possible to 'remember' smells too, since I have never forgotten the wonderful aroma of hot oil and steam. That experience must have sown the seeds for a love of railways which has stayed with me to this day.

Towards the end of the war we returned home, though not before spending some time staying with other relations who lived near Kearsley on the line from Manchester Victoria to Bolton where I saw my first LMS engines such as Class '5's and '2P' 4-4-0s. This association with the north-west was to continue in years to come, and, like many others, I took my last photographs of working steam in the same area in 1968.

After the war I joined the fabled Ian Allan Locospotters Club with its badge available in the colours of the then new British Railway's regions. Living on the 'Southern' I naturally went for the green badge and wish I still had it! Fortunately, I still have all my old *ABCs*, notebooks and diaries with details of the locos seen written in faded pencil on pages sometimes grimy with soot and oil.

Inevitably, I grew out of locospotting, though not before I had visited every shed on the Southern and many more on other regions. An invaluable source of help was Flt. Lt. Aidan Fuller's wonderful *British Locomotive Shed Directory,* with its incredibly detailed tours for 'doing' all the depots

Opposite Steam sheds were marvellous locations for photography, and sadly our private railways have yet to come anywhere near recreating the atmosphere of such places. Nine Elms could produce some striking images as is shown by the powerful picture of rebuilt 'Battle of Britain' class 'Pacific' No. 34077 *603 Squadron.* From a gap in the roof, sunlight is shafting through the steam and smoke to produce a wonderful effect which black and white photography brings out to the full. The 'Standard' tank, and rebuilt 'West Country' locomotives on either side balance the scene and are modelled by the light from outside the shed. The site of Nine Elms shed is now an impersonal fruit and vegetable market and it is almost impossible to believe that ranks of locomotives once stood in such dramatic splendour.

Basingstoke was always an interesting centre to photograph trains, particularly on summer Saturdays. In addition to the busy service on the main line to London, there were through trains to and from the Midlands and the North via Reading and Oxford, some worked by locomotives from the Western Region. In this photograph, taken from the east side of the line between Bramley and Basingstoke in the winter of 1960–1, a smartly turned out Bulleid set is hauled by 'Hall' class 4-6-0 No. 5901 *Hazel Hall* .

in a large city such as Manchester. Without the benefit of the directory, I remember trying to find the entrance to Patricroft one Sunday afternoon, though the high concrete coaling tower and the pall of smoke from the locomotives were clearly visible some distance away. Often sheds were a long way from the nearest station, but fortunately the directory gave walking times (sometimes as much as 45 minutes, assuming you did not get lost en route!). Annesley, on the former Great Central, was an example of an isolated shed for which a map reference was given.

I took my first railway photograph on September 8 1950 at Feltham shed, showing Class 'S15' No. 30506, which happily is still with us on the Mid-Hants Railway (at that time you had to carry your National Identity Card when visiting a shed and prove you had come by rail – quite right too!). I used the family Box Brownie to start with and then a simple folding camera. All things considered the results were reasonable, even if I did have to balance the camera on pieces of coal in shed yards when poor light required a time exposure. I still have all the negatives from those early days, taken using Ilford Selochrome or the more expensive FP3 film which came in a distinctive blue box. I dearly wanted to take action pictures, but the cost of a camera to do so was beyond my means until 1954 when I bought a Zeiss Nettar camera with a f4.5 Novar lens and shutter speeded to 1/250 second. With this equipment I was at last able to take moving trains, provided they were not going too fast.

In those days every male was liable for National Service at 18 and my call duly came in 1955. I was eventually posted to the Communications Squadron of the 2nd Tactical Air Force at RAF Wildenrath in Germany, where I worked as an engine mechanic on such venerable aircraft types as the Anson and Dove. Life at the squadron was almost like being in a busy shed with aircraft instead of locomotives. It was a constant struggle to keep the Ansons serviceable, as they all had their own quirks. The two harassed flight sergeants who shared the 24-hour running of the squadron had their direct equivalent in a shed master. When a 'kite' broke down or would not start, one of the 'Flights' would race out of the office shouting, 'engine mechanic!'

In the mid-1950s the railways in West Germany were almost exclusively steam operated, though the first diesel-hydraulics (basically the same as the later Western Region 'Warships') had made their appearance. There were still many reminders of the war such as bomb-damaged stations, dumps of derelict locomotives and battered ancient six-wheeled wooden coaches on the local trains, often hauled by a Class '38' 4-6-0. Germany was *the* place for photographic equipment, and even this soon after the war their camera industry had made a rapid recovery, although high-quality makes were very expensive and in short supply. In Dusseldorf I was able to buy a secondhand Zeiss Super Ikonta fitted with an uncoated f3.8 Tessar lens and Compur Rapid shutter. I also briefly used a pre-war Contax fitted with a f2 Sonnar lens, but the film transport proved unreliable. I remember how the lining of the case smelt

It is just before eight o'clock at Goudhurst station on the lovely Saturday morning of June 10 1961. My brother and I have travelled down on my Li 125 Lambretta scooter to take pictures on the Hawkhurst branch, and despite this being the last day of service, we are the only non-railway people on the platform. 'C' class 0-6-0 No. 31256 is arriving with the 7.40am train from Hawkhurst, whilst 'H' class 0-4-4T No. 31350 is waiting to cross it with the 7.35am train from Paddock Wood. Both engines are from Tonbridge shed. The 'C' class loco is passing the level crossing on the A262 road which leads up a long steep hill to the village high above the station. Nowadays there is no trace at all of the branch at this point and the station has long disappeared, The branch, which was just over 11 miles long, never enjoyed a good service and was poorly used, especially since most of the stations were sited well away from the villages they were supposed to serve.

The high curving roof of the 'Eastern' section side at Victoria station provided a good backdrop for this 1958 picture of an 'H' class 0-4-4T on the empty stock of a train from the Kent Coast. The misty weather and the light streaming into the station have provided the right conditions to give depth to the picture. Happily, in 1996 the station roof remains unchanged and it is quite possible to repeat this shot, though of course the train will be an electric multiple unit. The 'Night Ferry' sign in the background is a reminder of this service, which made its last run on October 31 1980. In the 1950s the sleeping car train left Victoria at 10pm and arrived in Paris (Nord) at 9am via the Dover-Dunkerque train ferry. The 1952 1st class return fare was £21 15s. 0d. (£21.75). How times have changed with the opening of the direct 'Eurostar' service to Paris and Brussels.

I always liked to include people in my railway pictures and this 1966 one has become quite well known. It was first published in my book *Steam Into Wessex* and shows my son Richard (then aged two) on a gate with his teddy who shows signs of surprise at the passing of the train hauled by a rebuilt Bulleid 'Pacific'. The location is on the north side of the line to the east of Winchfield station on a lane off the A323 road. The misty conditions have created the right contrast between the dark foreground and the lighter background. The gate and tree are still there, though the former has been replaced by a less attractive tubular metal model and there is much more vegetation on the lineside, making a similar picture difficult to take today.

strongly of cigar smoke, exciting the imagination about the camera's past life during the war! The Super Ikonta was a great improvement on the Nettar and served me well during the time I was in Germany and for visits to Belgium, Holland (where there was still working steam) and Luxembourg.

Returning to the UK in mid-1957 there was a great deal to photograph, and the large-scale closures of the Beeching era were, as yet, unimagined. My first love was the Southern and its many branch lines such as the incomparable one from Axminster to Lyme Regis. Fortunately, there was a regular Sunday excursion from Waterloo to Axminster and Exeter, ideal for visiting this branch to enjoy several hours photographing the Adams 4-4-2Ts which worked it. Photography was made so much easier by the generous issue of lineside photographic passes by the Southern Region which cameramen of my generation have cause to be so grateful for.

Ever keen to improve my photography, but still remaining faithful to roll film rather than 35mm, I bought a Voigtlander Bessa II in 1959 – 'the camera with the wonderful lenses' as the Voigtlander advertising said at the time. The lens was a very sharp coated Color Skopar with a Synchro Compur shutter. I later sold it for a similar Bessa II with a five-element Color Heliar lens, and used it for many years. Today, this camera, in mint condition, would sell for about £500!

My photography up to around 1960 had been fairly conventional, but increasingly during the following years when I visited all parts of the country in search of steam, my approach became more varied. Like some others, I tried to take a more imaginative approach to railway photography, to show steam locomotives, and the trains they operated, in all weathers, set against the rich diversity of sheds, stations and the many other interesting structures which existed at that time. The people who worked and travelled on the railways were important too, some of my most valued pictures from this era depicting shed and footplate staff, passengers, and of course the omnipresent locospotters.

In the 1960s I was fortunate enough to win a Bronica 6cm x 6cm single lens reflex camera in a national photographic competition. This piece of equipment was far more expensive than I could have afforded to buy myself, and helped me secure more ambitious and technically difficult pictures. The bright focusing screen made composition much easier, while the splendid f2.8 Nikkor lens and the top 1/1000 second speed of the focal plane shutter ensured that pictures of even the fastest trains of the day would be sharp. Sadly, however, the design and build quality of the camera was not of the best, eventually causing problems such as a sticking mirror or complete jamming when the shutter release was pressed, so I eventually sold it.

Colour photography in the working steam era was tempting, of course, but there were serious drawbacks. For example, the speed of films was slow (such as 64ASA for the Kodak Ektachrome I used), the cost was high, and many of the locos were so dirty that colour film was wasted on them. Despite these difficulties, I did secure a small number of nice colour transparencies using the Bronica or a 6cm x 6cm Super Ikonta camera fitted with an excellent coated Opton Tessar lens.

The four-and-a-half mile long Hayling Island branch, which ran from the main line at Havant, was famous for two things. First, the attractive bridge where the line crossed the channel between Langstone on the mainland and Hayling Island, and second, the LBSCR 'Terrier' class 0-6-0Ts based at Fratton (Portsmouth) shed which worked the frequent service. A parallel road bridge also crossed the channel to the east of the line and this formed a perfect location from which to photograph trains, especially towards sunset. This picture shows a train crossing the wooden bridge against a beautiful evening sky, not long before the line closed in 1963. To the right is the signal box controlling the swing section of the bridge, which could be opened to allow high-masted vessels through. Today the bridge has gone, though the concrete piers can still be seen and much of the branch can be walked along the 'Hayling Billy Coastal Path'.

97

It was always very enjoyable to make a trip to the Isle of Wight in the days of steam. As the boat from Portsmouth Harbour neared Ryde there was a great sense of anticipation, often heightened by the sight of puffs of white steam from a locomotive in the Pier Head station. On summer Saturdays, three trains at Ryde Pier Head would connect with the boat from Portsmouth Harbour, to Shanklin, Cowes and Ventnor. In those days, although there was a car ferry service, the majority of holidaymakers came by train and had to bring their luggage with them for the week or fortnight stay, but any large items would be sent as luggage in advance. In this animated scene at Sandown taken in 1962, a train has just arrived from Ryde. The travellers, eager to begin their holiday, are sorting out cases and bags before going off to find their guest houses and hotels. Unless they can afford a taxi, there may be a fair walk in front of them since the station was sited some distance from the seafront on the western edge of the town.

The passage of time has proved that Kodak film was the right choice, since there is little detectable change in the colour of the transparencies even today.

From the earliest days I have carried out my own black and white processing. I started by making contact prints using the dressing table in my bedroom as a work bench, which was hardly the ideal working environment. Nevertheless, this was a good introduction to more advanced work, and those early contact prints still survive in the albums I put together at the time. Nowadays, I have a proper darkroom with two enlargers which enable me to handle any size of negative from 35mm to 6in x 4in glass plates. I derive tremendous satisfaction from making black and white prints, and the ones I made for this book are no exception. It is a great thrill to print negatives for the first time, many taken in the 1950s and 1960s, or, using modern resin-coated paper, improve on prints made in earlier years. I have always felt that it is important to compliment a fine camera lens with a high-quality one for the enlarger, so I use the six-element Schneider Componon in three focal lengths to give optimum results.

Whilst the 'Glorious Years' of steam have long passed, I take as many railway pictures as before, though the scope and range of steam photography is now sadly very limited in comparison to the years up to 1968. On the other hand, colour photography has come into its own with a vast improvement in rendition and the speed of the film, so in good weather I tend to take transparencies rather than black and white. I still sense, though, that black and white is 'proper photography', for there is nothing to beat a fine print, be it of the modern scene or of days gone by.

One pleasant aspect of present-day steam operation is the running of charters, where photographers hire their own train composed of the engine of their choice with appropriate coaches or freight wagons. This idea was started in a small way a few years ago but has now grown to become an important part of the activity of many dedicated railway photographers. There have been several especially memorable charters, some for the bad weather they were run in, or for operational problems! One of the finest was with two unrebuilt Bulleid 'Pacifics' on the Swanage Railway, which was blessed with cool clear air and bright sunshine. The resulting pictures were magnificent. On such days there is nothing better than to enjoy the company of fellow photographers, laugh at the good-natured banter, and reminisce about those wonderful 'Glorious Years' and the pictures we might have taken!

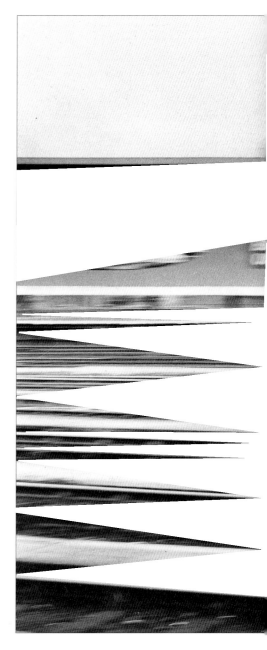

Panning pictures (that is, swinging the camera round to follow the movement of the subject) can be very satisfying under the right conditions. I must admit that after I developed the film and printed the negative, this picture was rather more striking than I anticipated. Using my Voigtlander Bessa II camera I have set the shutter on 1/100 second and followed the Standard Class '5' round as it coasts through Clapham Junction with an up train from Bournemouth. The loco is sharp whilst the sense of movement on the wheels and motion has been retained. The bonus is of course that the static British United BAC 1-11 jet on the hoarding is nicely blurred and gives the impression of speeding past the Class '5' – I doubt whether I shall ever achieve such an effect again!

Jim Carter

Opposite 'Britannia' meets 'Britannia' at Frodsham on June 10 1963. This shot was taken from the fireman's side of the footplate of No. 70027 *Rising Star* while working the 12.10pm Bangor-Manchester Exchange. No. 70044 *Earl Haig* approaches Frodsham station with the 1.35pm Manchester Exchange-Llandudno express as Patricroft fireman Peter Flack takes a breather. Nos. 70043 and 70044 were delivered new from Crewe Works in June 1953 and fitted with the Westinghouse Dual Braking System. Compressors attached to each side of the smokebox made it impossible to fit smoke deflectors and these locomotives were tested on coal trains as well as normal passenger workings on the LM region. In appearance they resembled a plumber's nightmare and as a footplateman I wasn't over impressed with their performance generally. I found rebuilt 'Patriots' and 'Royal Scots' better to work on.

During my childhood I was surrounded by railway lines and coal mines. My father worked at Clock Face Colliery, St Helens, and from my bedroom window I could see the pithead gear of Sutton Manor Colliery. From the end of Bentley Street where I lived, one could see the main line from St Helens to Widnes, beyond which were the access roads to Clock Face and Sutton Manor Colliery Sidings.

In those days (mid-1940s) steam engines were commonplace and a part of everyday life, much like present-day bus services. I was fascinated with steam locomotives, as was my younger brother Colin. We spent most of our time watching LMS freight, coal, local two-coach passenger services and the local colliery shunting engines. After a while we became aware that there were bigger and faster engines, not all that far away from where we lived.

I recall Dad taking us to St Helens Junction station, the first occasion on which we had ever seen a steam train at night, a vision I will never forget. The fireman was hard at work and the glow from the firebox reflecting on the escaping steam lit up the whole station. We were able to get close enough to the engine, which I remember as being large and green, probably a 'Scot' or a 'Jubilee', and to feel the vibration of the departing train through our feet. A week later, Dad took us to Lea Green Station, on the Liverpool-Manchester line between Rainhill and St Helens Junction stations. As we waited, he told us that the train would be doing a mile a minute. I couldn't imagine anything travelling so fast, until we saw a dot in the distance up the line towards Rainhill and in seconds a big green engine came thundering by, heading for Manchester. Two green express steam engine experiences within as many weeks! Although I couldn't have been much more than ten years of age, I was in no doubt where my future lay: on the footplate of these BIG steam engines.

It was only a matter of time before brother Colin and I became real 'train spotters', kitted out with Ian Allan's *ABC*, London Midland Region loco-spotters' book, and a set of wheels each to go with it – bicycles. Now there was no stopping us, we were well and truly hooked, and Lea Green, being so close to where we lived, became one of our favourite places on the Liverpool-Manchester line.

Every picture tells a story and sometimes the story is more interesting than the picture.

This shot of Patricroft Driver Reg Lawrence and Fireman Peter Holgate on rebuilt 'Patriot' No. 45525 *Colwyn Bay* at Leeds City station was the last kind of photograph that I had in mind when I booked on at Patricroft one summer Saturday in 1959 to relieve the Manchester Exchange bank engine crew. With a fully loaded camera and on a bright sunny morning, I was hoping to get a shed-full of photographs of the early morning activity around Exchange and Victoria stations. My driver was Jack Taylor and our engine was an ex-Midland Class '2P' No. 40671, which was standing by the side of the shunter's cabin at the east end of platforms 4 and 5. We hadn't been on the engine more than ten minutes before instructions came to gass up to assist an overloaded Liverpool Lime Street-Hull express as far as Leeds. Eventually the train rolled into platform 5. We hooked on and were away over the Pennines to Leeds and the trip passed without incident. After arrival, we ran through Leeds City station tender first, to turn our engine for the light engine run back to

Manchester. We could smell hot metal, and it turned out to be a hot axle box on the tender. No. 40671 was left at Farnley Junction shed for repair and we were sent back 'on the cushions'. My driver, Jack, boarded the train, but as there was half an hour before departure time I wandered up the platform to see which engine had backed onto the train. No. 45525 *Colwyn Bay* was an Edge Hill engine and I was invited onto the footplate for the trip back to Manchester. Peter was the oldest hand fireman at Patricroft and next in line to take the two-day test to drive steam locomotives, so Reg put him in the driving seat. Six coaches was a fairly light load for a Class '7P' engine and with only Huddersfield and Stalybridge stops to Manchester, Reg decided that the time was right to have a go at Marsden bank. In those days nine minutes was allowed for the descent from Marsden into Huddersfield and the challenge was to try to climb Marsden bank in less time. With the regulator handle up into the cab roof Reg and myself fired in turn continuously from a dead start at Huddersfield and No. 45525 passed Marsden station in seven minutes. What a trip to remember!

However, before long we realised that we were seeing, more often than not, the same engines time and time again. Eventually we found our way to the West Coast Main Line at Winwick Junction where, for the first time, I saw a Stanier 'Pacific', No. 46231 *Duchess of Atholl,* and this was when my love affair with these 'Coronation' class 'Pacifics' began.

During the late 1940s we paid regular visits to Winwick where the best of the London Midland express engines were to be seen, including some of the Stanier 'Pacifics' in blue livery. Also at this time, three North Eastern Class 'A1' 4-6-2s, No. 60159 *Bonnie Dundee*, No. 60160 *Auld Reekie,* and No. 60161 *North British,* were regular performers on the Birmingham-Glasgow expresses.

Of course, we had excursions to other locations on our trusty bikes and I recall a trip to Ditton near Widnes during the summer of 1951. We had only been there a few minutes when we heard a chime whistle, coming from the Runcorn direction, and 'Britannia' class No. 70015 *Apollo* cruised past down the bank towards Liverpool. At that period No. 70015 must have been almost new. Shortly after, another new sound caught our ears, emanating from the same direction, and this turned out to be English Electric No. 10001. Everything was happening so fast – it was a great life for young engine spotters.

School summer holidays were utilised to earn a few bob, by working on local farms picking peas and potatoes, to pay for film and to buy train tickets from St Helens Shaw Street to Wigan North Western, where we tried to photograph the busy summer Saturday traffic. At Wigan, in addition to the regular 'Duchess'-hauled trains, there were relief trains and Blackpool excursions, plus the traffic working in and out of Wigan Wallgate, the latter

This shot, taken from inside the roundhouse at Crewe North, is just an everyday scene. It shows the handsome proportions of the 'Coronation' class 'Pacifics' from a rear camera angle. I was continually drawn to 5A where Stanier 'Pacifics' could be photographed from any viewpoint and in any lighting conditions, in their home environment. Although I don't regard this as my best effort at Crewe North, it shows what sort of photographic opportunities were on offer during the early 1960s. No. 46256 *Sir William A. Stanier F.R.S.* and a 'Black Five' provided a lead into the main subject No. 46232 *Duchess of Montrose*, which was on the 70ft turntable prior to working a northbound express later that day. The camera used was an Ensign Autorange, exposure was 1/125 second at f5.6, and the film was Ilford FP3.

best observed from the south end of Wigan North Western station. There were endless photographic opportunities, but the only camera I had was a half-share in a Kodak Box Brownie, totally inadequate for the job of recording fast trains, or even slow ones if it comes to that. Those early opportunities soon passed, gone forever.

In my last year at Robins Lane School the shed yard at Sutton Oak was visible through my classroom window and I was more interested in what was happening in the shed yard rather than my classwork, which often got me into trouble. That year, from summer 1951 to summer 1952, I became a regular, albeit unofficial visitor to Sutton Oak shed and regularly had my collar felt by the shedmaster, Mr Hargreaves. On one occasion I asked him if he would put my name down for a job in the footplate grade, as I was only fourteen. He told me that he didn't want to see me hanging around the sheds any more and to 'come back when you have left school and bring your report with you'.

My last day at school finished at 12 noon, by 12.10pm I was knocking on his door, report in hand. Mr Hargreaves promised to send in my application and the following week I was asked to report for a medical in the medic coach in the Oldham bays at Manchester Victoria. Dependent on my medical, I would be notified by letter if I had got the job. For weeks I was on pins, waiting for the letter to arrive, yet each day passed and no word. As usual, during holidays, I got myself a job working for a local farmer picking spuds in a nearby field. One day my brother came running, waving like mad. 'Jim, a letter,' he said, panting, I opened it immediately, and yes, I had got the job. Happy as Larry, I picked up my gear and shot home, without even bothering to collect my spud pay. So my working life began one Wednesday morning at Sutton Oak, starting at 8am as an engine cleaner, and never had I been so happy in my entire life.

By this time I had a better camera, a Kodak Stirling, folding type with eight

With Threlfall's Cook Street Brewery as a backdrop in the early 1960s, two Stanier 'Jubilees' meet. No. 45650 *Blake* runs towards Manchester Victoria with the 8.10am from Blackpool as No. 45661 *Vernon* threads its way through the curves between Deal Street signal box and Salford station with part of the morning service to Glasgow and Edinburgh, the 9.30am from Manchester Victoria. This train joined with the 9.43am from Liverpool Exchange at Preston to depart at 10.30am and No. 45661 had Shap and Beattock to tackle before the train was split at Carstairs, with the rear portion of the train for Edinburgh and No. 45661 going forward to Glasgow Central, arriving at 2.50pm. This shot was taken while I was working on the Manchester Exchange banker with my faithful Autorange camera, using a shutter speed of 1/400 second at f8 on Ilford FP3 film.

exposures on 120 film, a top shutter speed of 1/60 second and a maximum aperture of f6.3. It was good enough for shooting engines standing in bright sunlight and I did have a limited amount of success with it, but the action shots were very disappointing.

After a year in the sheds doing cleaning and general labouring jobs I passed out for firing. We had no big express engines at Sutton Oak, therefore the only chance I had to fire the larger engines was when on loan to other depots, for example Patricroft, Warrington and Springs Branch. Myself and another passed cleaner, John Fryer, went on loan to Willesden during 1954 when the brand new 'Pacific' No. 71000 *Duke of Gloucester* and the latest 'Britannia' No. 70037 *Hereward the Wake* were in company with other locomotives on exhibition in the roundhouse. We were billeted in the Hampden Club Railway Hostel, between Euston and King's Cross, from where we could hear all the chime whistles coming from Top Shed and the station. All the top motive power from the various regions was on view and I made many attempts to photograph London's main line engines, but the shots taken were what one would expect from the glorified box camera I was using at the time.

During 1954 I moved to Widnes, on promotion from passed cleaner to fireman in the bottom shunting link. From the various shunting yards around Widnes, Edge Hill 'Princess Royals' could be seen, blasting up and running down Runcorn Bank with London or Liverpool trains. There were some good photographic opportunities here and I was on the point of selling my Hornby 'Duchess' and all my other railway modelling bits and pieces in order to buy a decent camera, when I received my call-up papers for two years' National

Stanier locomotives at Speakman's Sidings, Leigh, on March 10 1964: once again the practice of carrying a camera at work had paid off. This is 'Black Five' No. 44808 with Driver Dick Richardson and passed Fireman Bill Tonge. The '8F' was manned by Driver Tom Jones and myself. We were standing in the sidings of Bedford Colliery for over two hours waiting for the NCB loco to make up our train. Six loaded wagons at a time were shunted onto our brakevan to form half the train and the rest were placed in the next road. When the operation was complete, the two coupled Stanier engines were gassed up and backed on to the front half of the train. Then we had to draw out on to the main line and back on to the rest of the train. This manoeuvre gave me enough time to take a few photographs from Speakman's down home signal. Rolliecord VA camera, 1/500 second at f8 on FP3 film.

Right One Monday morning, January 21 1963, I booked on with Driver Frank Hulme at 5.30am to travel as passenger from Patricroft to Diggle in order to relieve a freight train from Mirfield and work it forward to Salford. There was only a dusting of snow on the ground when we left Manchester but more had fallen at Diggle over the preceding weekend. The relief point was the shunter's cabin near the signal box and Frank had his dancing shoes on, so we made a brew in the booking office-cum-porter's room, which can be seen to the right. Control informed us that our train was still in the sidings at Mirfield and wasn't expected to move for some time, so I decided to have a mooch around the station. The south lines were packed with frozen snow up to platform height and after a few minutes I heard a rumbling sound coming from one of the three tunnels. Next moment two engines emerged from the westbound single tunnel and ploughed into the hard-packed snow between the platforms. Cobs of frozen snow were flying all over the place and the engines were brought to a temporary stand, which gave me the chance to get my camera out. The engines in this shot are a 'WD' 2-8-0 and a Stanier 2-8-0 coupled together, tender-to-tender, and both fitted with ballast ploughs.

Service. I was unfortunate enough to take part in the Suez landings in 1956, and after the two longest years of my life, I was only too happy to be back on the shovel again.

Upon my return to Widnes shed, things were different; a lot of work had been lost and it seemed only to be a matter of time before the depot closed. A decision had to be made about the future, as my urge to work on the main line steam engines was stronger than ever. I wanted to get amongst the Stanier 'Pacifics', so I applied for a grade move from Widnes to Crewe North. After two unsuccessful attempts to move to 5A a third application was made late in 1958, with Patricroft Depot as a second choice. There were vacancies at Crewe North but the line of promotion was the rule of the day. Any passed cleaner to fireman took priority over an 8C, fireman to fireman move, and I had used up my 8C move going from Sutton Oak to Widnes.

On March 9 1959 I started work at Patricroft where, during the first week, I fired on two 'Patriots', two 'Jubilees', and a 'Royal Scot' working the 5.10pm Manchester Exchange-Windermere express. It was from then on that I really got into railway photography.

The best of my glorious steam years had passed without a decent shot to show for them so I invested £15 in an Ensign Autorange folding camera, fourteen exposures on 120 film, a top shutter speed of 1/400 second and a maximum aperture of f3.8. I know that £15 doesn't sound like a lot of money these days, but in 1959 it was more than a week's wages! When folded up the

Below After taking the photograph on the left, and learning that I had two hours to kill, I decided to make the most of this opportunity to take some more snow shots, so I set off walking westwards. Although it was bitterly cold the sky was clear and the sun was strong. After taking some snow plough shots I found myself nearer to Saddleworth than Diggle. I had been standing on the platform at Saddleworth station for over half an hour when I heard the sound of a three-cylinder engine hard at work and I soon forgot all about my frozen fingers and wet legs as 'Patriot' class No. 45545 *Planet* came into view. The locomotive was making up for lost time with the late-running 9am Liverpool Lime Street-Newcastle express over Saddleworth viaduct. No. 45545 had been brought into service by Edge Hill depot to replace a diesel found to have a frozen train heating boiler. After the passage of No. 45545 I joined my driver on a DMU back to Manchester, booking off at Patricroft at 1.30pm without handling a shovel all day, but a better day's work had been done with the camera! Rolliecord VA, 1/500 second, f8, Ilford HP3 film.

During the early 1960s, English Electric Type 4 diesels were taking over some of the WCML express work and Stanier 'Pacifics' were finding their way on to the North Wales Coast Line more frequently. From Patricroft we had rosters which took us to Chester and Holyhead where there were ample photographic opportunities. The 7.52am from Manchester Exchange was a good job for me, arriving at Chester at 9.17am, then light engine to Saltney to work a mixed freight train back to Patricroft. It was normal to be waiting for a path to Saltney at Chester No. 6 box when the 9.20am Crewe-Holyhead express was due. This was a train I always had my camera ready for, as more often than not it was hauled by a 'Coronation' class 'Pacific'. On the morning of June 23 1962 this train was hauled by No. 46256 *Sir William A. Stanier F.R.S.* and this shot shows it westbound after clearing the tunnels. The camera used was an Ensign Autorange with a shutter speed of 1/400 second at f5.6 using Ilford FP3 film.

camera fitted neatly in my overall pocket, and wherever I went, the camera went too. During 1960 a lineside pass was acquired so I could photograph steam locomotives in my spare time in addition to my work, but it was while at work that most of the best photographic opportunities arose.

Six 'Jubilee' class locomotives were allocated to Patricroft and although we had no Class '7P's, a steady stream of rebuilt 'Patriots', 'Scots' and 'Britannias', all on regular turns from other sheds such as Edge Hill, Carlisle and Holyhead, were to be seen at Patricroft. Nor was it unusual for the odd Stanier 'Pacific' to drift our way.

I always allowed myself at least half an hour before booking on in order to take a walk round the shed with my camera to see which of the bigger engines were in good photographic positions. On many occasions I had a few shots in the bag before booking on!

Sometimes, firing in the top passenger links became frustrating, as, for example, when working double-headed trans-Pennine expresses in daylight with unusual combinations of motive power, such as 'Jubilee' and 'Scot', two 'Jubilees' or 'Patriot' and 'Scot', when only the odd quick shot could be taken from the footplate. I recall countless occasions praying for a signal check so that I could take a shot in open country. There was never much time at stations before departure, for there was far too much to do: gassing up, hooking on, putting the buffer beam lamps right, more gassing up and watching out for the right away signal. When the light was right there were times whilst blasting up Marsden Bank (the Patricroft men's Beattock) that I would rather have been at the lineside with a camera in my hands than on the footplate.

There were, however, some good jobs for taking photographs in the passenger links that I looked forward to working: one each to Leeds and Liverpool and two to Chester. The 6.40am Manchester Exchange, all stations to Leeds, returning with the 8.45am Newcastle-Liverpool Lime Steet which had worked to Leeds powered by an Eastern 'Pacific', is one that particularly comes to mind. We worked this train forward at 11.29am, always utilising a Patricroft 'Jubilee', and as there was over two hours to kill before departure I would photograph the morning action at Leeds City station yard.

Another of Patricroft's rosters was to relieve an early morning, ex-Leeds express, at Eccles and work it forward to Liverpool Lime Street, then light engine to Edge Hill for servicing – coal, water, clean the fire and smokebox, and turn the engine – prior to working the 3.50pm local passenger to Manchester Exchange. Here again I had two hours' leeway before the time came to draw off shed. So having the camera in my overall pocket I proceeded to take advantage of the opportunity to photograph the wide variety of express engines that were to be found in the shed yard.

The 7.52am, all stations Manchester Exchange to Chester and back with a through freight from Saltney to Patricroft, was one of my favourite jobs. Once at Chester station it could take anything from one hour to two hours after being released from one of the bays to travel the short distance to Saltney via the triangle, No. 4, No. 5 and No. 6 boxes. Long periods of time were spent in the morning queue of light engines waiting for a path to Mold Junction or Saltney at Chester No. 6 box. Consequently, the chance to shoot some of the best LM express steam power, and Western Region locomotives working morning passenger trains, was not to be missed.

One week's work that could be made into a good photographic session was the Holyhead-York cattle train. For this, a Patricroft crew were booked as

Stanier Class '5MT' No. 45156 *Ayrshire Yeomanry* was moved to Patricroft when Edge Hill shed closed in early 1968. In the last week of steam operations from the depot my job was midnight shed man, dealing with any loco movements during the night. I had already decided to mark the closure of Patricroft sheds with a series of night shots of No. 45156 which had arrived on shed just after midnight on Thursday of the last week. After disposal, No. 45156 was moved from the ash pit into the shed where I set about a one-man engine-cleaning session that lasted more than two hours. The camera used was a Rolliecord VA twin lens reflex, set up on a tripod on the back of the tender of a dead 8F, set on B/time exposure at f11 with a lockable cable release attached. I had a small plastic flashgun and a pocket full of Phillips PF1 flash bulbs. There was little available light and the lamps in the sidings had already been turned off forever. It was no easy task locking the camera shutter open and climbing from the tender in almost total darkness.

passengers to Chester, on the 4.30pm Manchester Exchange-Llandudno Club Train, to relieve the cattle train and work it back home. On lovely, sunny, summer days when I was on this turn I travelled to Chester on the 7.52am from Manchester, spending four hours photographing steam-hauled trains between the tunnels, and No. 6 and No. 4 signal boxes, to Chester General station. I would phone Patricroft shed to check that the cattle train was running, prior to the departure of the 2.10pm train back to Manchester. If the cattle train wasn't running, I could catch the 2.10pm. When it was running, I carried on shooting until the arrival of the 4.30pm from Manchester, then teamed up with my driver, put my camera away and worked my way home on the shovel.

There were jobs with booking on times in the small hours of the morning, 2, 3 or 4am, which meant finishing time was before noon. On those longer summer days when the light was right, I would try and get to Crewe between 1pm and 2pm, where my photographic 'Duchess' jobs would start at Crewe North sheds. Crewe Works always provided a good variety of steam locomotives to photograph, between the Paint and Erecting Shops. Then, on my way to South shed I would have another look around 5A, where I always finished up having a good photo session shooting the Stanier 'Pacifics' arriving and departing. These jaunts could be hard work after a shift on the shovel, but were well worth the effort. Although I never managed a transfer to Crewe North in order to regularly work these 'Pacifics', I certainly got amongst them with my camera.

My last visit to 5A was on September 25 1964. After working a freight from Patricroft to Mold Junction, I was working back as passenger and on arriving at Chester I left my driver to continue his journey to Manchester alone, while I travelled to Crewe North where No. 46256 *Sir William A. Stanier F.R.S.* was being cleaned up to work the last 'Coronation'-hauled train to Carlisle the following day. I emptied my camera taking shots of No. 46256 inside the roundhouse. Saturday September 26 1964 was a very sad day for all 'Coronation' class 'Pacific' enthusiasts. I photographed her at Warrington and that was the last time I saw a Stanier 'Pacific' during steam days. On my way home I felt a great loss; it was as if I had been to a funeral to witness the passing of a dear friend. In later years I could never bring myself to photograph steam engines being cut up in scrap yards.

My best lineside experience was the day I met Eric Treacy for the first time; it was on the curve between Chester No. 6 and No. 4 signal boxes. He looked more like a platelayer than a man of the cloth and I found him to be a friendly and modest steam-loving enthusiast. In subsequent years our paths crossed on several occasons and in many locations, one of which springs particularly to mind. This was at Leeds City station during the early 1960s and the train in question was the 8.45am Newcastle-Liverpool Lime Street, which arrived in Leeds at approximately 11.10am, to be worked forward from Leeds to Liverpool by a Patricroft 'Jubilee' on which I was booked fireman. As we reversed onto the train Eric was on the platform, and after a quick word prior to departure at 11.29am, black smoke was arranged on approach to Eric's chosen photographic position. The last time I saw him was at Bishop's Lodge, Wakefield, in 1972. I feel very honoured to have known him.

I no longer turn out for main line steam jobs after having my collar felt on a number of occasions by the BT police; the last steam specials I saw were at Llandudno Junction on April 13 1993. Nowadays I confine myself totally to photographing steam on the East Lancashire Railway. Finally, to quote my old 'Shap mate' Derek Cross, 'there is no such thing as a perfect photograph', when you think you have taken one the 'if only' factor creeps in. And how right he was. I am still trying!

Don Rutter

As a small boy, one of my lasting memories was the clockwork Hornby train set I received one Christmas. In those days it was nearly every small boy's dream to become an engine driver and little did I then know that I would actually realise that dream. I'm not sure when the actual golden days of steam were, and if truth be told, I was probably only involved in the latter stages of its demise, but to me, all the railway memories are golden. Nowadays, when I see some of the beautifully restored steam engines pulling a train over the Settle & Carlisle line, I become very nostalgic, for my mind goes back to the time when I worked at the Rigby Road Motive Power Depot in Blackpool. I spent some of the happiest days of my working life there, although I must say that the day I started work at the MPD in 1953, I wondered what on earth I had let myself in for.

It was a cold, dank and misty winter's morning, just coming light as I made my way into the shed. It was so gloomy and dimly lit by the gas lights, and thick acrid smoke enveloped everything. There was the noise of hissing steam and the clanging of shovels and fire irons as crews prepared their engines. Other crews were signing on and checking the board on which was chalked what engine was working which train, and where it was stabled in the eight-lane shed. Another busy place was the store where firemen drew shovels, headlamps and a bucket containing tools and detonators, while the driver got a large can of oil, all of which was part of engine preparation. A group of young lads assembled outside the foreman's office where we were introduced to the charge-hand cleaner, Teddy Ash, a small bespectacled figure with only one arm. He spoke to us about what we were required to do and then showed us round an engine, indicating which parts we were to clean.

We were split up into groups of four, given a bucket of cleaning oil and rags, and each group was allotted an engine to clean. It was cold, dirty work and we spent a lot of time drinking tea in the canteen, always being dragged out by Teddy Ash to get us back to work. Over the coming months we learned about the engines and how they worked. We learnt the rule book off by heart until, one day, we completed the test to become passed cleaners.

Shifts were worked around the clock and we longed for a firing turn, even if it was only on the pilot engine, shunting carriages in and out of Central station. We used to love listening to the engine crews going off duty, telling us of some of the dramas they had encountered, some of them spending hours talking at the end of their shift. The shedmaster was Pat Hoskins, but we never saw much of him unless we had done something wrong. In those circumstances we received what was known as a Form 1. For example, it could ask a driver to explain why he was five minutes late arriving in Manchester. One humourist once replied: 'We were finishing our Murraymint, the too-good-to-hurry-mint!'

I received a Form 1 just after I was married, which asked me to explain why I was late to work every morning the previous week. I replied: 'Just got married, the spirit's willing but the flesh is weak'. The most important thing was not to receive a Form 3 which meant suspension from duty. I think that you had to murder someone for that! Gradually we spent less time cleaning engines and eventually I became a fireman, but promotion was slow at Blackpool and, after the summer season finished, there was a lot of surplus manpower with nothing to do but clean engines. Volunteers were asked to go on loan to London, which was a good opportunity to earn some extra money and get some firing turns.

A group of us went, Doug Dunstan, Eric Davies, Peter Harvey, Jim Parkinson, Charlie Cooper, Johnny Jones, Barry Ferguson, Charlie Hogarth and myself. We stayed in the railway hostel in Polygon Road not far from Euston station. I went on loan three times, once working at Devons Road (Bow) and twice at Kentish Town MPD. What we liked best was going to work for only three hours, disposing of six engines and then signing off. It was hard, dirty work, but one got stuck in with the reward of finishing work early. With a group of lads on loan from Liverpool we had some great nights out in

The author, Don Rutter, at the controls of a Stanier 'Black Five' on a run to Manchester. Although still only a fireman, some drivers used to let you take over to gain experience. It was only after ten years on the footplate that I became a passed fireman, after a rigorous three-day examination by footplate inspector Wilf Marsden. I never did get an 'official' driving turn as, just after I 'passed out', Dr Beeching announced the closure of Blackpool Central station. The end came on the last day of the 1964 Illuminations, Sunday November 1st. I was off work at the time with a broken wrist, after a blow-out on my motorbike. Tommy Houghton was on the pillion that day, unharmed. While on sick leave I received my redundancy papers, which I signed. Tom is still working, I am now retired. There must be a moral there.

the West End, visiting places like Humphrey Littleton's and Chris Barber's jazz clubs.

A lot of the lads I started with had to do National Service when they reached the age of 18. I remember going for my medical at Fulwood Barracks near Preston with a few other workmates. It was at the time of the Suez crisis and during the medical we were asked if we would like to be deferred until after the crisis, or alternatively get called up and get it over with. For some reason they let railway workers have a deferment and I asked to be deferred. I never did get called up, but a lot of my friends, who had not opted for deferment, were called up within three months.

As a fireman I was teamed up with Bill Davis and spent some time on runs to Liverpool, Manchester and Crewe. All of Bill's family were great railwaymen and I remember firing for his brother, Jeff, one day when he scared me half to death. We were bringing a coal train from East Lancashire and soon after leaving Preston on the fast line, a passenger train came alongside on the slow line. This was a challenge to Jeff, so he started to race the other train. He kept up with it as far as Salwick, and even now I can remember looking back at our coal wagons, swaying all over the place with coal bouncing off the track and our guard hanging on to his hand brake for dear life! Jeff slapped the brake on at Salwick and the passenger train shot away, much to the delight of all the passengers hanging out of the windows. Jeff said that we would never stop at Kirkham and started blowing the whistle for the signalman to give us a clear road. Luckily we got the road, shot across the junction and managed to stop on the incline up to Wrea Green. We then had to set back into Kirkham North sidings, where a white-faced Fred Whiteside tottered out of his brake van. The only thing he said as he passed the engine was: 'You barmy bugger!' I could not help but agree with his point of view.

On the electric turntable at Rigby Road MPD, Blackpool, Stanier 'Black Five' 4-6-0 No. 44819 turns before dropping on to the ash pit for fire cleaning, coaling, water tank filling and shedding. The stone building on the right was the pay office; on Thursdays a steady stream of railwaymen would collect their wages in a little tin can from Ernie Banks. The turntable was also outside the office of the shedmaster, Pat Hoskins. It was at Blackpool Central MPD, at the turn of the century, that another railway aristocrat in the making was quietly working away. As part of his training the young Nigel Gresley was running shed foreman at the MPD.

A scene that would get you the sack nowadays. I am on the left, with driver Jack White, enjoying our lunch in the 'Yorkshire House', Manchester. After working an early morning train from Blackpool to Manchester, we went light engine to Newton Heath MPD to turn the engine, clean the fire, coal and water, then down to Red Bank sidings for our stock. We had an hour to spare before dropping down to Manchester Victoria, so we climbed up the signal gantry and over the wall for a pub lunch. Jack White was badly hurt when he struck his head on the signalbox structure when running into Southport one day; he has never worked since.

Opposite A classic seaside steam scene. A pillar of smoke rises skywards as Stanier 'Black Five' 4-6-0 No. 44947 eases out of platform 3 with a Manchester express around 1960. The coming of the railway to Blackpool in the nineteenth century transformed it from a small seaside village into one of Europe's busiest holiday resorts with 12 million visitors a year. The town's most famous landmark, the 518ft high Tower, was officially opened at Whitsuntide in 1894. To this day the outline of the filled-in platforms are still clearly visible.

Our main runs were to Manchester, but a lasting memory was the time we were working the 7.55am to Crewe out of Central station. Travelling between Kirkham and Preston on the slow line we caught up with the 8.18am out of Blackpool North on the fast line. This was the train that Violet Carson travelled on, from her home in Bispham to the TV studios in Manchester, where she played Ena Sharples in *Coronation Street*. I could kick myself to this day that as we ran alongside her compartment there she was grinning and waving to us, and I had not got my camera with me.

Probably our most exciting run was the 5.03pm from Manchester Victoria. First stop was Blackpool South, due in at 6.09pm, but with a good road it was possible to arrive at 6pm. All I can say is that it was a great test of the driver and fireman's ability. The hardest part of the journey was out of Manchester and up the bank to Atherton and Dobs Brow. We could then relax and enjoy the run down to Chorley and Preston. From Kirkham the route was over the 'New Line' or 'Marton Line' as it was known. There was no greater feeling as the run down to South Shore and the view across to Blackpool Tower. Braking from Watson Road signalbox I often thought we would never stop at South Shore station. The run from Manchester was often done in under an hour and it was nice to hear some of the passengers congratulating us as they passed the engine.

Certain drivers could make the fireman's life hell by flogging the engine unnecessarily. One of the worst to fire for was George Hewitt, known as 'Conker Bollocks' (the railway was very strong on nicknames). Strong in arm, all the firemen hated going with him for he used to flog the engine unmercifully – such was the ferocity of the blast in the firebox that the coal was sucked off the shovel. One hot summer's day I was with him on the branch line from Fleetwood to Kirkham. At the latter station, a porter came up to us and said that there were reports that we had set fire to every field from Fleetwood. George laughed and said: 'What do you want me to do, sit on the smokebox and catch the cinders?' Exit porter. He was the only driver that I got stuck for steam with while going up the bank to Chorley on a Manchester express. George is dead now, God bless him. Characters like him made the railway a joy to work on.

Another incident that put the wind up me was the time I was firing on a coal train from Rose Grove, near Burnley. Coming down the bank from Houghton to Bamber Bridge we started to run away as the brake was not able to hold the weight of the coal wagons. The driver, Joe Seddon, gave a special whistle to

the signalman to let him know we were running away, hoping that we would get a clear road. We managed to stop eventually, but it was a frightening experience wondering what was ahead of you. One other bad experience was one morning when I was firing on an up express to Manchester. Running down the bank from Bolton we suddenly saw a figure stood across the rails and looking over his shoulder. The buffer struck him in the back and he flew through the air. I had to give a statement to the police but only my driver had to attend the inquest. Every bone in the man's body had been broken.

Some of my last years were spent in the top link working to London, Crewe, Liverpool and Manchester. Most of my trips to London were on English Electric 2000 HP diesels (Class 40). We worked the 5.05pm from Blackpool Central and were due in Euston at 11.05pm. If we were lucky we could arrive before 11pm and dash out for a quick pint before the stock was drawn off. We used to leave the vacuum pipe off the train after we had unhooked, just to pinch a few more minutes.

I remember one nightmare journey in thick fog, with driver Harry Parkes, when we arrived at Euston four hours late. We lodged at Camden but it was almost impossible to sleep as there were shunting movements outside the lodge all night. The rules stated that one could not work again until 12 hours rest had been taken. This meant that we had to work a different train back to Crewe.

Driver Dick Fenton oils the big end of Stanier 'Black Five' No. 44927 in platform 4 before departing with the 2pm to Manchester. Whilst driving a DMU from Manchester to Blackpool he narrowly escaped being killed when a broken rail end was thrown up by a train passing in the opposite direction. It crashed through the front window and bounced into the train. Sadly, such was the force of the impact that a passenger sitting in the second compartment was hit and killed.

118

Walking down the line from Central station back to Rigby Road MPD. My driver, Bill Davis, passes the time of day with his brother George Davis. We were finishing our shift after working the 7.55am train to Crewe, then returning to Blackpool on the 'cushions'. This train was worked with an English Electric 2000 HP diesel and was used to train footplatemen. In the front cab would be five people, two trainee drivers and the instructor, Ernie Bellamy, my driver and me. In the back cab there would be four firemen learning how to operate the Stones train-heating boiler. My driver Bill Davis had a lucky escape from death. One early morning coming to work on his motor bike, a telegraph wire brought down by gales, sliced through his thick railway jacket and cut his throat down to the windpipe. Found lying in the road he was taken to hospital and stitched up.

The engine was a 'Duchess'. I had never fired one in my life and was advised to keep the back corners of the firebox full of coal, but somehow we struggled through. I remember how impressed I was when I saw all the headboards in the stores at Camden shed. What price would they all be worth today?

We were rostered to do two trips to London in one week every month, with two rest days in between. This earned me £20, the most that I ever earned on the railway. My regular driver became Alf Chew, a nice and easy-going person. Most of our trips to London were with Class 40 diesels and as I was getting near to becoming a passed fireman, Alf used to let me drive.

On Sunday mornings a group of us would meet in the lodging house near Blackpool Central station. These LDC meetings were led by Bill Langley, an ex-footplate man and running foreman at Rigby Road MPD. He used to throw every possible incident at us that might happen while working a train and we came to know the rule book backwards. The time came when I spent three days with Wilf Marsden, a bowler-hatted footplate inspector. Two days were spent on the rule book and one day driving on

Stanier 'Black Five' 4-6-0 No. 44733 backs onto the train in platform 4, prior to working an express to Manchester. In platform 5 can be seen a DMU, which spelled the end for steam train operations. To the right can be seen the toilet block which is still in use today. In front of the toilets is the old engine that was used to steam heat the carriages. It was reported that the income received from the toilet block paid the station's rates bill! Blackpool Central station came into being when the line from Lytham was extended in 1862, with the station opening on April 6 1863. At first it was known as Hound's Hill and was renamed Blackpool Central in 1878.

the footplate. You cannot imagine my joy at being told that I had passed. I was now qualified to take charge of a steam engine – it had taken ten years. I never did get a driving turn, for the clouds were gathering. Dr Beeching was axing Central station and no one could believe it. Then I had an accident on my motorbike and broke my wrist. During the three months that I was on sick leave I was given my redundancy papers. I had married in 1960 and I was getting fed up with the shift work and low pay, so I decided to take the £100 redundancy money and used it as a deposit on a mini van. The final act came when Blackpool Central station was closed on Sunday November 1 1964.

So there you have my railway days in a nutshell, from the Hornby train set to a passed fireman. I have lots of happy memories and feel privileged to have played a small part in the 'Glorious Years' of steam. I still have that Hornby train set to this day and I would not part with it for the world.

Most of my photographs were taken on a Voigtlander Vito B using Adox KB17 and developed in Rodinol. My main interest in photography was when I used to take the camera on my fell-walking expeditions. The odd times that I took the camera on the footplate was to photograph my drivers.

So the few negatives I have been able to find are very rare. When the British Railways Staff Association was formed we started a photographic group, meeting in the club rooms at Hampton Road. We even had a dark room there, one of the keenest members being Keith Hodgson, the stationmaster at Squires Gate. It was not until I left BR that I joined the Blackpool & Fylde Photographic Society and took my hobby more seriously.

Here's a tale you might like. I was frying egg and bacon on the shovel one morning when a gentleman asked me if he could come on the footplate. He watched me cooking my breakfast and remarked how good it smelt. 'Would you like a bacon sandwich?' I asked. After he had eaten it he said, 'That's the best bacon sandwich I've ever tasted.' After a while he asked what we do when taken short on the footplate. 'We use the shovel,' I said!

I hope that people reading this book will enjoy sharing some of my memories. I still see some of my old railway mates, though alas a lot of them have gone. I would like to dedicate this chapter to them.

Fireman J. P. Smith returns the electric turntable back into its normal position at Blackpool Rigby Road MPD. Behind is Spen Dyke signalbox, built in 1901 and containing 120 levers. The signalman must have been very fit to shift the manual levers at the height of the summer season. The name Spen Dyke was taken from a peaty-coloured stream which drained water into the sea near the Foxhall. The town takes its name from a dirty-coloured 'pool' that Spen Dyke ran into, hence the name Blackpool.

Michael Mensing

The Glorious Years: just when were they? This must be a matter for individual perception, and I suppose my own view of the pinnacle of railway supremacy would be that now-remote era between about the turn of the century and the First World War. For that matter, to those of us old enough to remember everyday steam operation of railways in Britain, that age didn't seem so remote. Many of the locomotives we saw were at least direct descendants of that era; a few even survived from the late nineteenth century! These latter relics, though, owed their survival to quirks of fate like low axle-loading for severely restricted branch lines, or long superannuated use on local or lightweight goods work.

Any book, however, must reflect strongly the era in which it is published, and only a few of us, contributors or readers, can have memories going back much before the 1930s. Those too were 'Glorious Years' in some ways, but very short-lived. By the time the grouped 'Big Four' (GWR, LMS, LNER and SR) had resolved some of the profound traumas of cohabitation with traditional rivals, the 1939 war swept them into a vortex of neglect and underinvestment which left them ill-equipped to face the post-war upheavals of nationalisation and the revolution in our lifestyles wrought in only a few decades.

So, as a mere 62 years old, my photographic view of British steam is definitely post-war, and whether or not those were 'Glorious Years' must remain a debatable question. The fact is that the pace of change was overtaking steam operation, and by 1955 the BR modernisation plan spelled the death of this labour-intensive style of traction. In the end, this plan turned out to be too little, too late, and an indecent haste to get rid of steam at, literally, any cost by 1968 resulted in a hugely wasteful scrapping of steam locomotives. Concurrent with this, of course, was a hasty investment in a plethora of untried diesels. The one great-value-for-money component of that policy must have been the host of diesel multiple-units, so cheap and effective and in some cases even surviving into the 1990s.

Arising from that steam massacre, it bothers me now that so many of our preserved steam locomotives (and now, even, newly built ones!) reflect only the last stages of their design in this country. Historically, the preserved steam scene is very unbalanced.

I was really a less-than-dedicated railway enthusiast originally, being merely interested but not widely knowledgeable as a child; only from the age of sixteen did I take a more detailed interest. Having been brought up within sight of a GWR main line, my instinctive preference is for the locomotives of that company. This is nothing more than prejudice, though, and any machine that will boil water and thus convert heat into motion is a constant source of fascination. I never joined the band of true fanatics, however, whose enthusiasm manifested itself largely in countrywide visits to steam locomotive depots, collecting every number in sight and grabbing a few static photographs if their budget would run to the luxury of a camera.

In these days of universal automatic cameras, extremely pliant film characteristics and staggeringly accurate mass-production of colour prints, it is instructive to remember the difficulties under which the photographer laboured in the 1950s. Nearly all cameras were German, either pre-war or slightly inferior products of a reviving industry; supplies of these were severely restricted by Exchange Control regulations, and prices were thus quite high. Several British companies tried to exploit the situation by making copies or

On Sunday August 30 1959 I travelled from Birmingham Snow Hill to see the Talyllyn Railway. Having read about the preserved MR 'Compound' 4-4-0 No. 1000 on an SLS special, I travelled into the city early to call in at New Street. The weather was sunny, allowing a photograph while waiting, but, when No. 1000 drew into Platform 7, I could scarcely believe my eyes! Outside a museum I have never seen a locomotive so immaculately painted and polished. Although the contrast was beyond the range of 1959 colour film, I took two slides of this spectacle, then this second black and white shot as she left for York and Doncaster.

The rebuilt 'Royal Scot' 4-6-0s came late to the Derby-Bristol route, when the English Electric diesels (Class 40, as they became) freed them from West Coast Main Line use. No. 46137 *The Prince of Wales's Volunteers (South Lancashire)* (phew!) was employed on the Saturday 10.05am Bournemouth (West)-Derby on July 1 1961, seen here leaving Platform 7, Birmingham New Street. She was three-quarters of an hour late, but that was probably due to summer Saturday traffic congestion rather than to any deficiency of the locomotive or crew. The carriage examiner with his hammer, casual onlookers and number-collectors add welcome human interest. It is worth recalling that by this time the 2,500hp 'Peak' diesels were already taking over on this route.

Taken on August 8 1964, this view is of Birmingham New Street some months after the start of rebuilding. Work on the Midland side was well under way, but at least there was some traffic still using it. The only sign of work here on the Western side is the support for the relocated footbridge at right and top. The main girder visible is one of the supports for the utilitarian asbestos platform canopies built in the 1940s after the Luftwaffe did for the elegant overall roof. LMS '4F' 0-6-0 No. 44123 of Gloucester Barnwood is at Platform 5 with a westbound parcels, which may well have been a Midland Division working diverted here to relieve the Midland side of the station.

near-copies of the German models; many of these were of excellent quality, but equally expensive – certainly beyond my pocket! The interchangeable lens, even the single-lens reflex, were unknown to the majority, and the zoom lens was not to be generally available until the Japanese, in their turn, virtually took over the market.

1954 saw my 21st birthday, and a principal present was a Brownie 127 box camera – my introduction to photography. Previously my brother had been the photographer in the household, but on his marriage that mantle seemed to fall on me. Neither he nor my parents, by the way, had any interest in railways, so there had been no childhood influence on my preference for the subject. Very soon I was learning the basics of photographic principles and trying out my new acquisition on passing trains on the nearby GWR Birmingham to Leamington main line. A few films made it clear that I needed something a little better than a box camera, which had, however, given me a good introduction to basic techniques. A new but reasonably cheap German $2\frac{1}{4}$in x $3\frac{1}{4}$in folding camera with a maximum shutter speed of 1/200 second and an enticingly fast f3.8 lens was my next step up the equipment ladder. That lens, though, showed its limitations at anything wider than about f8, and a still higher shutter speed became essential because then, as now, I was most attracted by moving train photography. That camera's inability to hold the film flat was a further drawback.

Next came another German camera, $2\frac{1}{4}$in square, with, at last, 1/500 second and an f2.9 lens. This was an improvement, and by that time I had developed a great liking for the square format. Other railway photographers for whom I have the greatest respect and admiration cannot abide this shape, but after many years' involvement in both taking pictures and their subsequent enlargement, I remain convinced that it is the easiest. There is no question of making the scene fit the frame, and subsequent prints can utilise just as much or as little of the sky or foreground as suits the case.

I took a further step forward in 1956 with a Voigtlander Perkeo – only an f3.5 lens, but a real beauty – and that camera did Trojan service until its demise from sheer overwork in 1964. Meanwhile, in 1958, against my principles but attracted by the larger format, I had bought a shop-soiled Voigtlander Bessa II (2¼in x 3¼in) camera, for which I had great hopes. I made good use of it for a year or so, but somehow the lens didn't have the Perkeo's 'bite', and after consorting briefly with a couple of other 2¼in x 3¼in models and falling back on the Perkeo, I bought myself a very secondhand Hasselblad.

I used this camera for a couple of years to very good effect. It was by no means perfect, but its top shutter speed of 1/1000 second and fine Tessar lens produced pretty consistent results. In the end it too had to go because (1) it always had slightly uneven shutter coverage at top speeds and (2) it didn't take

This view is of the west end of New Street station on April 23 1959. Platform 10 is on the right and the short No. 11 bay behind the left-hand columns, with Fowler 2-6-4 tank No. 42340 waiting to leave with the 5.32pm to Redditch. Before that, Stanier Class '5' No. 44814 will depart with its train, the 5.25pm to Malvern Wells. This train was a regular working for an LMS engine through to Malvern, in Great Western territory – presumably a legacy of the former Midland Railway's own route to Tewkesbury and Ashchurch, which had its own station on the branch until closure of the Malvern to Upton-on-Severn section. Despite breaking many traditional 'rules' of railway photography, this picture fascinatingly conveys the atmosphere of old New Street.

Compared with New Street, Birmingham Snow Hill was an airy, spacious station, with four long through platforms, four north-end bays and two centre through tracks. On one of these stands '7200' class 2-8-2 tank No. 7247, waiting for the road on an up freight, mostly empty iron-ore hoppers, on September 25 1960. These massive engines were rebuilt from Churchward's 2-8-0 tanks, by lengthening the frames and extending the bunker to increase their range, and were seen in small numbers on this route. No. 7247 was shedded at Banbury, the focus of a lot of iron-ore traffic due to the extensive Oxfordshire ironstone quarries at nearby Wroxton. Trains of iron-ore to the steelworks at Bilston were a familiar scene on this stretch.

kindly to the Kodak film base which I had taken to using. For some reason this Hasselblad couldn't be relied on to hold Kodak film flat! I was an early experimenter in colour transparency film, incidentally, and as materials have improved over the decades, so an increasingly large proportion of my output has been in colour.

By 1964 the Japanese had become a significant force in the camera market and I 'went 35mm' with a Nikkorex single-lens reflex and interchangeable lens. In fact, I never bought a second lens, but by using one body for colour and a second one for black and white I could make it a dual-purpose machine. This camera also had the annoying habit of intermittently failing to hold the film flat, but it saw me through to 1975 and still finds occasional use for copying purposes.

More recently I used a $2\frac{1}{4}$in square Bronica, and now a Mamiya 645. Again, interchangeable magazines enable me to use one camera for two purposes, and the general standards of equipment quality have improved beyond recognition in a couple of decades or so.

Enough of cameras, though. These days, in any case, the emphasis in any hobby is, I believe, placed far too much on technical equipment. A lot of simple satisfaction can be obtained from using the most modest technology, within

Above Snow Hill station could accommodate many spotters, and the north end was favourite, with good views of every movement. This is the up side, with Platform 8 and the pedestal-mounted North signalbox at left and bay No. 9 centre. 'Modified Hall' 4-6-0 No. 7908 *Henshall Hall* is drawing parcel vans from the adjacent Platform 10 on July 18 1959. The slow demise of this station after the withdrawal of through services in 1967 was painful to see. Following the diversion of Stourbridge services and closure of the GW route to Wolverhampton, the site was levelled by 1978. The new station, and the Metro line to Wolverhampton, bear little relationship to the old railway.

Below I have always regarded the Great Western 'Castle' as one of the handsomest locomotives of my era, and the truth or otherwise of this assessment may be judged from this action portrait. No. 5060 *Earl of Berkeley* is seen heading the up 'Inter-City' on April 24 1962, just south of Acock's Green & South Yardley station, Birmingham, with a mundane backcloth of the rear ends of the rows of houses in The Avenue. The one disfiguring feature of this engine is the double chimney, however laudable its capacity for further increasing the free-steaming character of the class. On the 'Kings' it seemed quite in keeping, but its height and forward setting on a 'Castle' marred the graceful proportions.

its limitations, to achieve modest results. Certainly the cameras which I used in the steam era were well below top-of-the-range standards.

Whether or not the dozen years from 1956 were 'Glorious' ones, they contained my entire contribution to the photographic catalogue of British steam locomotives. Thus I am under no illusions regarding the minute scale of this contribution to the history of steam, or, for that matter, of railways generally. I have always been interested in railways as a whole, and when steam locomotion began to decline this did not deter me from photographing anything else that moved on rails. The scene today, however, is so lacking in variety, and lineside views are so restricted, that I take only a fraction of the number of photographs that I used to. Darkroom work, mostly printing the negatives and colour transparencies of thirty years ago or more, provides a lot of interest throughout each winter, however.

Let us not lose sight of the 'dirty' side of everyday steam engine operation in all our pleasant nostalgic memories of that era. The reality bore little relationship to the romantic image, and the hardy generations of men who built, repaired, cleaned, fired and drove these often obstinate and always challenging machines deserve our greatest respect. The sheer hard labour and skill required to urge, say, an LNWR 'Precursor' 4-4-0 with a 300-ton train over the gruelling miles from Euston to Crewe at an average speed of 45-50mph are of an order which nowadays is difficult to credit. Add to that the frightening amount of labour required to clean the engine, to prepare it from cold, to clean out the smokebox and firegrate – just for example – afterwards. All this was in working conditions which in this post-steam era would be downright illegal, so one can appreciate how far we have come in a few decades. In our own post-war times those squalid, primitive conditions for steam

This picture at the east end of the North Western side of New Street was chosen to convey something of the grimness of steam operation on a slightly misty winter morning. Steam leaking profusely, 'Jubilee' class 4-6-0 No. 45733 *Novelty* crawls into the short Platform 6 with stock to form the 11.10am to Glasgow and Edinburgh on Sunday February 19 1961. The dead-end platform extension on the right was often used (apart from train-spotting!) to back in the rear ends of trains originating from here, which otherwise fouled Platform 5. The Hasselblad was at maximum aperture here, and it does show! This, by the way, was the only occasion I ever joined an organised party to visit a locomotive works (Crewe). Never again!

operation were scarcely improved. It was therefore no wonder that the more modern surroundings and better wages offered by the motor manufacturers and other employers sapped the railway workforce, thus causing a vicious circle of deterioration in a labour-intensive industry. Those who loyally stayed on to carry the burden of steam working to the end, some with truly heroic enthusiasm, merit deep respect, though their day-to-day dedication and ordeals were not newsworthy, unfortunately.

The accompanying photographs, all taken in Birmingham, give only the merest hint of past railway operations in that city. If the emphasis is on New Street station, that is because it epitomises the revolution on the railway front; it was a place of multifarious views, and I spent many a Saturday afternoon there in the late 1950s and early 1960s. This was particularly easy because it was a 'walk-on' station, unusual in those times of universal ticket inspection. From the traveller's point of view, however, the place was a squalid shambles, and ought to have been replaced many years earlier. Snow Hill was a much more spacious and tidy station, and with a lot of freight traffic passing through there was seldom a dull moment. New Street, though, saw scarcely any freight.

My photographic style has always been of the unobtrusive kind. In steam days, tripods and suchlike equipment were not generally permitted on platforms in any case, and even a camera could arouse staff hostility; so my methods were those of a discreet bystander. In the few cases where people appear in my pictures, they were invariably unposed, and probably unaware of their inclusion. In any case, under the cavernous roofs of the Midland side of New Street station, I had to concentrate on holding the camera steady at exposures like 1/25 or even 1/10 second!

Johnson '2P' 4-4-0 No. 40332 looked rather decrepit by April 4 1957. Despite the 'standardisation' of the original design in Fowler's days, these engines retained their 7ft 0½in driving wheels; unlike the 6ft 9in version built in the misspent early years of the LMS locomotive department. At the east end of Platform 10, New Street, the fireman can be seen shovelling forward coal, for this old-stager not unusually worked the 5.45pm stopping train to Bristol fifteen minutes later. She is waiting for the 5.32pm to Redditch to leave before moving down Platform 10 – always ready to assist the latter train at the rear, should it stall in the tunnel. The greasy rails in the tunnels at each end of the station were a locoman's nightmare, especially for the westbound standing start.

Neville Knight

My interest in railways started during school days in the early 1940s when I used the train from Didsbury to Chorlton-cum-Hardy. It attracted others too but school finishing time did not slot in with the 3.55pm from Manchester Central to Sheffield, which was timed at Chorlton at 4.04pm; to miss this involved a very lengthy wait for a later train, and in order to connect with the desired service I was allowed to finish school five minutes earlier than everyone else! A late finish meant a hectic run to the station; in those days most trains ran very much to time. The engine was usually LMS 'Jubilee' class No. 5573 *Newfoundland* – a '5X' from Millhouses 19B, but now and again it was a 'Compound' or an occasional Class '5' off the Midland Division. The school grounds overlooked the railway near Chorlton Junction and a regular performer during the dinner break was the first Class 'B1', No. 8301 *Springbok*. This working was via Guide Bridge (off the GC Woodhead line), the locomotive returning usually tender-first light engine to Gorton shed. Another regular engine was 'Compound' No. 1008 of Leicester shed with a stopping train routed, like most, via Stockport Tiviot Dale. The ex-shops engines from Gorton Works used the Fallowfield line via the triangle at Hyde Road; they tended to be LNER 'O4s' or the odd 'J11', some simply lettered 'NE' in plain black.

It was a period of shortages, financial particularly, and in those days I had no camera. Later, as my thoughts turned to photography, my early days with a camera were largely experimental. Most families had a conventional box camera and I once managed to get hold of flat sheet film, which was cut in total darkness with a razor blade to fit inside the back of the box camera. The camera was then taken immediately to Heaton Mersey shed but the results were a disaster; the film fogged through the red window, which of course was only intended to show a number on the backing paper on Ortho film (such as Selochrome) and not a fast Pan unprotected emulsion!

Heaton Mersey shed was really two sheds in one: near the gate adjacent to the river were all the best LMS locomotives, and beyond were housed the less interesting ones of the LNER. It was an easy shed to look round if permission was granted first by the foreman. Inside it was very dark and smoky, especially on a Sunday evening when the LMS 2-6-2Ts, '2Fs', '3Fs' and many '8Fs'

were simmering in the gloom. The LNER side had about three roads holding mostly 'J10s' and a few 'N5s', along with one or two 'B9s', the mainstay of the CLC services from Stockport to Warrington and Liverpool.

The best viewing location was almost beneath the Midland lines where the Cheshire lines passed underneath. Some days American troop specials seemed to pass through almost one after the other from Liverpool; they were worked by 'B7s' from Gorton, but 'K3s' were not unknown along with the odd 'J10'. To the American servicemen it was their first impression of England and they were prone to throw out coins (that could not be spent) and chewing gum or chocolate, the latter still being on ration. Above, was the local service from Manchester Central to Cheadle Heath and the fast St Pancras turns mostly worked by 'Jubilees'. In more recent years the M63 motorway was built, which will eventually form a motorway ring around Manchester (M60), and Heaton Mersey shed is no more. Gone too are all the trains from Tiviot Dale and the Midland into the city.

As time passed, I started to wind my own film on to spools from surplus material, a time-consuming and delicate job, but it did have its rewards, for it was better than nothing! Film was only obtainable as surplus RAF material; and this in 25ft rolls some 9in wide. Cutting this to size in a darkroom had its moments as you can well imagine; sore and cut fingers sometimes resulted in a blood-stained film, but as a rule it was possible to make some negatives, though none were prize winners!

A friend once showed me how to make postcard enlargements and I was allocated the 'wet job', using my fingers instead of tweezers – a terribly cold job in a darkened cellar. But the thoughts were implanted and some time afterwards a home-made enlarger emerged from the kitchen floor; this worked quite well, though good bromide paper was still not freely available. However,

A bright early spring morning at Garsdale on April 19 1954, where the train engine, LNER 'G5' 0-4-4T No. 67345, had already run round its two compartment coaches after working the first train of the day, the 7.15am from Northallerton. The 39¾-mile line via Hawes through Wensley Dale was typical of many branch lines, with lengthy waits at some of the intermediate stations. The enginemen's room at Northallerton, on the previous night, had a roaring stove and lots of hot tea, making it a pleasant place to chat away the early hours – while outside in the cold night air our 'G5' was simmering peacefully. Garsdale in those days was quite busy, but the Settle & Carlisle did not have the attraction that it has today.

The 'B17s' were familiar in Manchester from 1929 onwards with many being shedded at Gorton. The majority of the class were allocated to sheds in the Eastern Counties and worked services into Liverpool Street. However, they were shopped at various works including Stratford, Gorton and Doncaster. A party visit to Doncaster on January 18 1953 produced an ex-works 'B17' No. 61618 *Wynyard Park*, built as No. 2818 at Darlington in 1930 and named after the country house of the Marquis of Londonderry. Altogether there were 73 locomotives constructed between 1928 and 1937, as 2800-2872, from the works of North British, Darlington and Robert Stephenson. They became 1600-1672 between January 1946 and January 1947. In September 1937, 2859 and 2870 were streamlined. Ten locomotives were rebuilt at Darlington between 1945-9, to become Class 'B2'. No. 61618 was withdrawn from Cambridge in January 1960.

RAF glossy paper in large-size grade 2 or 3 could be located in the war surplus outlets in Manchester. When unwrapped, some of the paper was usually damp, damaged or fogged!

In the interim years I bought an '88' camera and later a nice Balda which had a remarkable lens, albeit f6.3, but the main limitation was the relatively slow shutter speed of 1/100 second, which gave no scope at all for action work. For a time I used an Ilford Sportsman and later I had a pair of Pentax SP1000 cameras, both with standard 50mm lens that could be fired off together when clamped to a piece of wood, which was useful if two action exposures were necessary.

In more recent years I have used 35mm film for both black and white and colour slides. I purchased a Gamer Enlarger, which was far better than many on the market after the war; it is a precision instrument, though my wife considers it most ugly. Despite this, I still use it! For many years I used mostly Grade 2 or 3 papers and I liked Kodak Bromesko, which had a sparkle all of its own. Today the majority of black and white paper on sale is Ilford Multigrade, which covers some five grades including half stages, a useful attribute with difficult negatives; one set of filters works just as well with almost any manufacturer's paper. I try and keep the developer hot, much warmer than recommended, as somewhere in the print should be a good black. Many people settle for grey photographs when a combination of correct grade of paper and correct development should give a satisfactory print. Nowadays, I use an electronic timer, which means that if more than one print is required, exposures will be identical. I never use processing solutions twice.

Night photography can sometimes look rather artificial, and it is not a process I would claim to be really proficient at. I did try using PF60 flash bulbs but I was not altogether satisfied with the results. I once tried flash powder ignited in a biscuit-tin lid, which to everyone's surprise, illuminated a 'C13' *and* the night sky of Barnsley! After that experience my night work was confined to available light, but it is hopeless if the subject is in almost total darkness.

My own colour photography nowadays is on Kodachrome; having tried most others I like K64 or K200 and the Kodak emulsions have stood the test of time without any fading, still looking as good as the day they were taken. I make sure, though, that they remain in darkness when not needed. A bag of silica-gel will keep out moisture, and if contaminated, these bags will dry off quickly when placed on a central heating radiator for a few minutes.

It is possible to copy black and white negatives on to positive film to produce transparencies. This requires a jig made out of cardboard. The original negative is placed in a window cut into suitable card that is hinged by masking tape to join the two sides together, forming a clamp so that the negative can be seen, with the upper section of the two halves secured by a bulldog clip to hold it firm. Next, the negative holder is placed between two short pieces of timber beading to hold the mask upright. From behind the negative, place a folded card at 90 degrees, which is then illuminated by a photo-flood, or better still, one at each side. The camera will need to focus on to the negative plane; this can be done with a set of extension tubes or close-up supplementary lens, the camera being retained on a parallel alignment. The film for copying is quite slow, and initially, bracket exposures might be necessary, but as a guide the film is about 10ASA. Metering is carried out 'through the lens' in the normal way, using any suitable shutter speed; 1/15 second being possibly the optimum. The film must be developed in a normal paper developer, as one would use when enlarging; the developer mix should be 1:3. Develop in a tank for around six minutes; extending beyond this period makes very little difference. Text books do not provide this information, but practice can provide slides of exceptional quality from old negatives. I have used this method to reproduce my own negatives of the Isle of Wight as transparencies and, although it needs some degree of patience, the results can be very rewarding.

My best period for photography on British Railways was the early to mid-1950s when there was such a huge and interesting range of locomotives, with

Built in 1925 (Beyer-Peacock No. 6209) as LNER No. 2395, Class 'U1' Garratt No. 69999 seen here on a 43-wagon 600-ton test train: the first of a series of trains which operated between Dewsnap Yard and Crowden on the former GC Woodhead line. The viewpoint is high above the former Manchester Corporation Woodhead Reservoir, and the photograph is dated October 11 1953. The tests were to determine the steaming capability of the locomotive which entered Gorton Works early in August 1952 for conversion to oil firing. After conversion, testing of the locomotive took place between October 1953 and early 1955. The Garratt went to Bromsgrove in June of that year, but the tests were unsatisfactory and the locomotive was withdrawn from Gorton in December 1955 and cut up at Doncaster. Most of the Garratt's life was spent on banking duties at Worsborough, and it was the LNER's largest locomotive, appearing in the 1925 Stockton & Darlington celebrations. The Woodhead line, electrified at 1500V dc in 1954, was eventually lifted beyond Hadfield and is now a footpath.

Left A Midland Railway '3F' 0-6-0 No. 43387 (9D) was the locomotive used on the final section of the Stephenson Locomotive Society and Manchester Locomotive Society rail tour on June 27 1953. The location is Harpur Hill, at the top of a 1-in-41 gradient, a bleak and windswept location on the Ladmanlow branch from Hindlow. The '3F' worked the train from Friden to Parsley Hay joining the former LNWR Ashbourne to Buxton line through Hindlow. The train continued a further 2½ miles, passing Stanley Moor Reservoir, and crossing the A54 Buxton to Congleton road, to terminate at Ladmanlow Goods. This was the second of the SLS/MLS tour trains; the previous one on April 25 of that year was hauled by '3F' 0-6-0 No. 43618. In December 1958 the LNWR Harpur Hill to Ladmanlow section was being lifted.

Bottom left Some of the rail tours of the early 1950s were very attractive, both from a photographic view point and for the lines they covered. The tour arranged jointly by the Stephenson Locomotive Society and Manchester Locomotive Society on August 24 1952 was one of them. From Manchester Central (now the G-MEX Exhibition Centre) this tour commenced with the last remaining Midland Railway '3P' 4-4-0 No. 40726 leaving Manchester via the former Derby line (now part used by Metrolink trams) over the now lifted route through Didsbury and Heaton Mersey to Sheffield Midland, with a photo stop at Chinley. The locomotive had been specially cleaned by enthusiasts at Trafford Park! Waiting at Cudworth was gleaming 'D20' 4-4-0 No. 62360, seen here against a background of 'post-war pre-fabs'. The tour continued behind No. 62360, which then took the former Hull & Barnsley line to Hull (Paragon).

Below Gotham, seen here on June 27 1953, with an 1889-built North London Railway 0-6-0T No. 58856 working a joint Stephenson Locomotive Society and Manchester Locomotive Society rail tour train on the Cromford & High Peak line between Longcliffe and Friden. Passengers were carried in 'open stock' and three brakevans. The four North London Railway locomotives were allocated to Rowsley shed, and rotated as required, one being spare. Access to the line for this purpose was via Buxton. The NLR tanks continued in use until the 1954-56 period, when Class 'J94' 0-6-0STs were considered as replacements. The final NLR 0-6-0T to survive was No. 58850, built at Bow in 1881 and withdrawn in September 1960. Today, as LNWR No. 2650, she has a new home on the Bluebell Railway in Sussex, being the locomotive used to recover some of the redundant track on the Ardingley branch, a once electrified line to Horsted Keynes.

much of it being pre-grouping stock. I did obtain a BR 'walking permit' which gave me unrestricted access between Woodhead and Manchester London Road, but eventually restrictions were imposed after the 1500V dc electrification programme was introduced.

Interest then moved over to some of the branch lines where it was much easier to get quite different photographs in sometimes very scenic locations. Unfortunately, Dr Beeching came along and destroyed so much so quickly that it was almost impossible to keep pace with closures. Time was at a premium and it was not until 1956 that I got my own car, an ancient Austin that boasted 22 previous owners! As the end of steam was in sight, vast withdrawals of engines took effect, and little remained other than dirty Class '5s' and '8Fs'. This, however, left another field almost untapped – miniature railways.

Here a whole new world emerged, along with so many new railways to see. Visiting them, I made many new friends whom I value greatly, and offering a few prints now and again helps enormously. If people are approached in a proper fashion I seldom have problems and it is really amazing just what is around. People like to show you what they have constructed and I often wish that I had the skill to do the same. However, miniature railways do have a rather different following to main line steam and they do not interest everyone.

Class 'C13' No. 67421 ready to leave Godley Junction for Glossop on September 28 1953. In the early 1950s the local passenger services from Manchester London Road to Glossop and Hadfield were largely in the hands of 'C13s' and 'C14s', but occasionally larger locomotives were used, such as 'J11s' or 'B1s'. When orders for new 'B1s' were delivered from Vulcan Foundry they were run-in at Gorton shed and they too could be seen on local services. Several 'B1s' were allocated to Gorton for use on the Sheffield Victoria, Hull and London services. Motor-fitted 'C13s' could also be found on Glossop trains, working coach first from London Road.

Overseas steam possibly falls within similar limitations, depending of course on where and what it is. Australia offers some scope. Even in Tasmania in 1982 I found a Beyer-Peacock 2-6-0, with Gorton works plates, working on the Don River line to Coles Beach. And this on Boxing Day, although there it is in the middle of their summer! I was offered a footplate journey on this immaculate locomotive. In Launceston City Park I found another Beyer-Peacock, a 4-4-0, now a resident of the children's play area and it still has a full set of maker's plates.

In 1975 I ventured to East Germany, then still behind the Iron Curtain, not really knowing what to expect. There was still quite a lot of steam, and some still survives on the narrow-gauge lines. These are worth a visit as they have a charm of their own, making them very photogenic. All went well until, for some reason, I was left at one of the International Hotels in Dresden. The German tour guide asked me where I was going and guided me across the town. 'Don't look round now,' she said, 'but we are being followed by the Secret Police.' This was real James Bond. Suddenly life took on a new meaning!

Godley Junction was situated between Guide Bridge and Dinting on the GC Manchester to Sheffield line. In 1954 it formed an interchange where steam could be replaced by electric locomotives to operate through the new Woodhead tunnel. The photograph shows LNER Class 'K2' No.61771 approaching Godley Junction working an eastbound Class 'K' freight in the summer of 1953. During this period some freights were piloted by the new Gorton-built electric 1500V dc locomotives. Adjacent to the 'K2' is No. 26005, a class later renumbered into the 76XXX series.

Eric Woods

The 'Glorious Years' started for me in 1932 when, at the age of 12, I acquired my very first camera. It was a Box Brownie and it cost my parents the vast sum of 12/6d (75p) at Molson's the Chemists in New Road, Spalding.

I wasted half of the exposures on my first film because nobody had told me that the single shutter speed of a box camera was not fast enough to stop the movement of even a slowly moving locomotive.

Soon I progressed to a folding camera, a Kodak Autograph which I purchased from the mother of one of my friends. This had two shutter speeds, 1/25 and 1/50 second but did nothing to solve the problem of photographing moving trains. Nevertheless, I used it to quite good effect on my early visits to the London termini.

It would be in 1936 that I invested in an Ensign Selfix whose top shutter speed was 1/100 second. Also it had a lens whose aperture could be varied from the maximum of f6.3. Although a large proportion of my pre-war railway photos was taken with this camera I was never really happy with it. The bellows tended to come unstuck and, as the missing rear ends of several tenders testify, the tiny viewfinder pointed to the right. So as soon as I could afford it I recklessly spent all of £5 on a really advanced camera, a Zeiss folding camera with a top speed of 1/125 second and a maximum aperture of f4.5.

After the war a Post Office colleague brought home from Germany an Agfa 'Billy Compur' which he had acquired in exchange for a packet of cigarettes. He sold it to me for £20. He made a handsome profit and I got a camera that lasted me until the end of steam in 1968 – and beyond. It is still perfectly serviceable.

My friends and I used to develop our films in a makeshift darkroom: a blanket pinned up over the window and door of the pantry and a one-candle-power lamp with a piece of red glass at the front for illumination. We were not too particular about developer temperatures and I lost at least one film when a solution which was too hot completely removed the emulsion from the celluloid backing. The wonder is that some of those early negatives are still fit to print, sixty years later.

I used to produce prints on so-called self-toning paper. On prolonged

exposure to daylight this gave a quite pleasant sepia print which was fixed in a hypo solution. Soon I was introduced to the mysteries of 'Gaslight' paper which had to be developed to produce a black and white image after exposure to artificial light. Exposure times were very hit-and-miss and I probably wasted as much paper as I used successfully. And I never really solved the problem of 'staining' or oxidisation.

In those early days the orthochromatic film that we used was not sensitive to red light and was oversensitive to blue. Consequently, red buffer beams came out black, the red lining on black engines disappeared, while white steam was invisible against a blue or (more generally) grey sky.

All this changed when a well-known photographer of the day, F. H. Gillford, came to Spalding to write an article on 'Spalding as a Railway Centre' for the *Railway Magazine*. He introduced me to the benefits of panchromatic film which, while it solved the problem of colour rendering, could not be processed at home by the time-honoured method of dish development in red light. We took our films to be developed by Syd Harrison the chemist, which meant that, for me at least, pocket money would not extend to having many prints made. I stored my negatives carefully against the time when funds would become available, and they survived intact until I returned to them after the

After unloading its train at platform 6 at Spalding, Beyer-Peacock 4-4-0 No. 26 has drawn its train forward as far as the long overbridge that spanned the goods yards and running tracks. The three coaches are a rare old mixture – a Great Northern six-wheeler, an ex-LNWR corridor 1st/3rd bogie carriage, and a non-corridor bogie carriage of NER origin. Old No. 26 was built in 1883 and so was 53 years old when I took the photograph. She was withdrawn from service a month or two later in November 1936. The brass cut-out numerals favoured by the MGNJR were elegant but not the easiest of characters to read from a distance. The similarity between a 3, a 6 and an 8 has misled more than one recent author into wrongly identifying the subject of a photograph.

A train for Sutton Bridge stands at Spalding's No. 1 platform, headed by Johnson 4-4-0 No. 078. Built by Beyer-Peacock in 1899 to a Midland Railway design this engine survived as LNER Class 'D52' to carry its new number and black livery until February 1938. All the MGNJR 4-4-0s received extended smokeboxes in the course of their careers, but No. 078 was one of a few that went one better and got an even longer extended smokebox. In my photograph it also sports the wide chimney (shorter than the dome) that was fitted to a few members of the class before the LNER took over the MGNJR locomotive stock in October 1936. The original vestigial cab roof has been extended, thereby producing, so one of the drivers told me, an unpleasant drumming sound at speed. The three-coach train appears to have a similar make-up to that of No. 26 in the other MGNJR photograph, namely, a six-wheeled van, an ex-LNWR and ex-NER eight-wheeler, but marshalled the opposite way round.

war. Since then I have, unfortunately, lost a fair number by trustingly lending them, usually to people who were 'going to write a book'. All too often the 'loan' has become permanent.

About forty years ago I invested in a simple enlarger and embarked upon the congenial task of printing the backlog of negatives. My degree of success was admittedly limited, but it was all good fun.

In the beginning, my photography was limited to the environs of Spalding station and shed, where we seemed to have the run of the place. Apart from those places, where locomotives could be photographed at rest, a favourite vantage point was the long footbridge that spanned the up and down goods yard as well as the running lines.

I must have been a dreadfully shy lad and was most embarrassed when one of the 'locals' passing by observed: 'Gret big lads, watching the trains go by. Ought to be at wuk.' Thereafter, and for quite some time, whenever a passer-by appeared I would pretend that I, too, was crossing the bridge and not merely 'watching the trains go by'. It was too bad if this occurred when I could see approaching a train that I wished to photograph. I'm sure that today's youngsters would be less sensitive to criticism!

By 1934 my horizons had begun to broaden. My parents bought me a little single-speed bicycle, and I and my friends, Len, Brian, Mac, Tommo and George, essayed the long ride to Essendine on the LNER main line. I managed to get a number of acceptable shots of stationary locomotives there, though Len's always seemed to be better. I even tried 'panning' my camera to beat the speed of a Gresley 'Pacific' or 'P2', with a modicum of success.

On one memorable occasion the down 'Flying Scotsman' train was hauled by the *Flying Scotsman* locomotive, and this nearly got us thrown off the station. We were well-behaved lads but on this occasion our excitement got the better of us and we went down the ramp to get a better view. Out rushed the stationmaster, probably alerted by the 'bobby' in the South Box. 'You might have been cut to pieces,' he cried. 'Ah,' said Brian, his eyes gleaming behind his spectacles, 'but what an honour – to be cut to pieces by *Flying Scotsman* himself!' There was no answer to that and, on promising never to go down the ramp again, we were allowed to stay.

Other cycle trips were to Peterborough, although we preferred to catch the 8.11am train from Spalding when funds permitted. This got us to Peterborough in time to witness the passage of one of the 'P1' goods 'Mikados' No. 2393, or No. 2394, on an immensely long coal train.

In 1934 I paid my first visit to London and achieved my ambition to see the 'Royal Scots' and 'Claughtons' that I had admired from photographs since childhood. I shall never forget the thrill of seeing my idols for the first time, and thought of it some forty years later when I had the same sensation on seeing some of the classical sites in Greece.

In those pre-war days one had to have written permission to photograph, even from station platforms. Only the Southern made an exception and when I applied for permission to photograph on Waterloo station I was told: 'Our engines will be pleased to have their photographs taken by you. All we ask is that you do not impede the working of the station.'

Later I got permits to visit most of the London motive power depots. It was on one of these visits to Willesden that I found the re-boilered 'Claughton' No.

On returning to Spalding from my first visit to London in September 1934 I was delighted to find the famous No. 4472 *Flying Scotsman* awaiting departure from a nearby platform at King's Cross in a perfect position for a photograph. In my opinion this view shows off to full advantage the classic lines of a Gresley 'Pacific', unsullied by such aids to efficiency as a double chimney, smoke deflectors and 'steam collector' dome: to say nothing of its present (temporary, one hopes!) dull green livery.

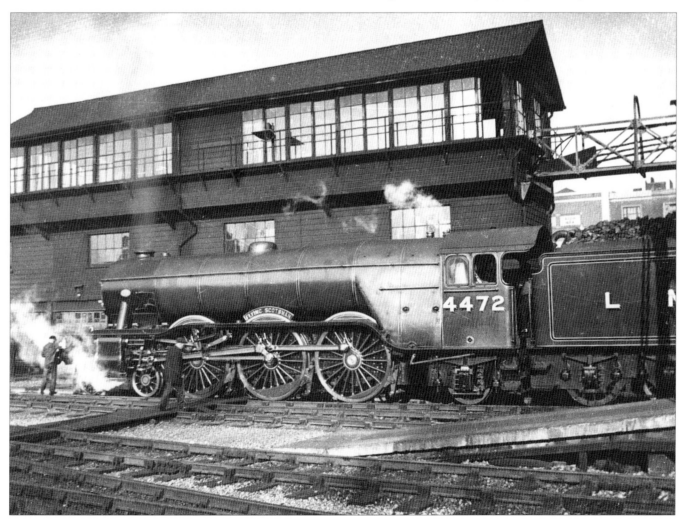

Right When the railways were nationalised on January 1 1948 no time was lost in arranging trials between roughly corresponding locomotive types of the four constituent companies. The test trains all seemed to arrive in Leicester at about midday, so by judiciously adjusting my lunch hour I was able to see something of what went on. I was thus able to photograph the GWR's *Witherslack Hall* at Central station, and the LNER's 'B1' *Oliver Bury* and the Southern's No. 34005 *Barnstaple* at the London Road station. My photograph shows the last named arriving with a train from St. Pancras – and I was the only person around with a camera! Of course nowadays one becomes accustomed to seeing preserved locomotives at work far from their homeland. The wonder is to see one on a line to which it really belongs.

Below In June 1950 a prolonged spell of convalescence enabled me to spend some time beside the Great Central line near Birstall where we were staying with my friend Syd Newton, son of the celebrated photographer S. W. A. Newton who, at the turn of the century, had photographed the construction of the Great Central's London Extension. By 1950 the 'B17s' with which Leicester enginemen had wrought such wonders in pre-war days had been reduced to more menial tasks. Here is No. 61650 leaving Belgrave & Birstall on a Leicester-Nottingham local, with a decidedly mixed bag of carriages. The name of the locomotive which the little girl was apparently so intent on reading was *Grimsby Town*.

6004 lurking in the depths of the shed and to my surprise the shed foreman had her hauled out into the sunshine for me. The same thing happened at New Cross shed when I wanted to photograph one of the Brighton 4-6-2 tanks. When I moved to St Annes many years later, the local enthusiasts used to assure me that 'the further north you go the more co-operative the shed foremen become'. But I, for one, have the happiest of memories of London railwaymen.

In 1936 a weekend excursion from Spalding to Blackpool, organised by the local Labour Party, enabled me to see a little of the L&Y – 2-4-2 tanks, a 'Baltic' tank and six of the remaining 'Dreadnought' 4-6-0s. But my most ambitious pre-war safari was with a RCTS visit to north Wales sheds. I worked my night shift (2.50am to 11.15am) at the Post Office, caught the 2.31pm from Spalding to King's Cross behind rebuilt Ivatt 'Atlantic' No. 3279 and joined the party for a midnight departure from Paddington. We visited the Chester sheds, as well as Wrexham, Mold and Oswestry, getting back to London in the early hours of Monday morning. I caught the first available train from King's Cross back to Spalding, having subsisted for the weekend on bars of chocolate from automatic machines. Was it all worth it? Yes! I had seen and photographed such exotic strangers as 'Bulldogs', 'Aberdares' and a Cambrian Railway's 0-6-0.

This is the train from Bourne unloading at Essendine in 1951 shortly before the branch closed. When I first saw this train in the early 1930s the motive power was one of the elder Mr Ivatt's 4-4-2 tanks. Subsequently the old articulated twin-set, formed from the bodies of two GNR rail-motors, was seen in charge of 'J4' and 'J6' 0-6-0s and even a 'K2' 2-6-0 before ending up with one of the Class '4' 2-6-0s pictured here – the work of 'old' Mr Ivatt's son. Even after the closure of the Bourne to Essendine branch the ancient vehicles were not finished. I saw them at York in 1957 in a train from Scarborough behind a Standard Class '5' 4-6-0. The railwayman to whom I was talking was disgusted. 'No wonder folks are beginning to turn to the buses,' he said.

The war put a stop to that sort of thing. It prolonged the life of many old favourites, however, and on return to 'civvy street' there was a desperate rush to photograph some of them in their last days. Or there would have been if film had been available. Just after the war I considered myself lucky to get hold of some ex-RAF film (by means upon which I will not elaborate) – very fast, very contrasty and very grainy.

A move from Spalding to Leicester in 1947 gave me the choice of three stations and the excitement of the 1948 Locomotive Exchanges. Holidays in Scarborough, Dawlish, North Walsham and Barmouth enabled me to photograph trains in slightly more exotic surroundings during the next few years.

In those days a visit to another part of the country could be relied upon to produce something rich and strange. Some years ago a Post Office colleague, R. S. McNaught, wrote an article entitled 'The Joys of the Unexpected' for the *Railway Magazine*. I remembered this expression in August 1966 when returning from a holiday in Fife. On the outward journey we had a Stanier Class '5' from Blackpool to Carlisle, a diesel over the Waverley route to Edinburgh and another Class '5' from there to Kirkcaldy. I thought it would be great to have a similar journey back home, but the shrill whistle that heralded the approaching train did not belong to a Class '5'. To my amazement, round

In 1948 I was one of a small band led by the late Ray Tustin who got together to form the Leicester Model Railway Group and I had the honour of becoming the first Hon. Secretary. We paid several visits to places of railway interest, not the least of which was the locomotive testing plant at Rugby. On one of these visits it was a great thrill to find a 'Standard' Class '5' 4-6-0 on the rollers; and the sight and sound of this locomotive going 'flat out' while remaining stationary was an experience not to be forgotten. Note the Westinghouse brake pump on the right hand side of the smokebox. No. 73050 was one of two 'Standard Fives' that received this fitting for test purposes in 1953. This locomotive is now preserved on the Nene Valley Railway.

When I was told in 1954 that I was to be transferred from the Leicester Telephone Manager's office to the one in Preston, my first thought was, 'Shall I be able to get photographs of a Fowler 'Royal Scot', a 'Baby Scot' and an 0-8-0?' I did, and the 'Clan' class 'Pacifics' (for my money the best looking of all of the 'Standard' classes) were an additional and totally unexpected bonus. They turned up at Preston on a train that divided there for Manchester and Liverpool, and on the Fylde Coast line on summer Saturdays with trains bound for Blackpool. I managed to see all ten members of the class before they disappeared. Here is No. 72000 *Clan Buchanan* about to pass under the Highbury Road bridge at St Annes. On the other side of the bridge were the rotting remains of the steps that used to lead down to the erstwhile Gilletts Crossing Old Links halt. Even the pipes that used to carry the gas supply to the little halt were still in position.

the curve appeared the smiling face of Class 'V2' No. 60919. Unexpected joy indeed!

It is all a lifetime away. It must be five years since I saw even a preserved steam loco on a main line and I'm getting withdrawal symptoms! What would I not give to hear the syncopated beat of a Gresley 'Pacific' roaring up the bank beyond Essendine with 16 or 17 carriages on its tail; or the plaintive whistle of an Ivatt 'Atlantic' gingerly threading the gloom of Peterborough station with the 'Queen of Scots'.

Those were the days! For me the 1930s were really the 'Glorious Years'; and what came after was rather a sad anticlimax, with post-war dilapidation, mass withdrawals and hurried dieselisation hanging over our heads. Even those days were glorious, compared to today's endless procession of multiple units of one sort or another and 'privatised' trains in liveries that the late C. Hamilton Ellis would have described as 'loudly screaming vulgarity'.

I'm glad to have my memories and lots of photographs to refresh those memories. The 'Glorious Years' were good while they lasted!

To celebrate the centenary of the Doncaster 'Plant', the two preserved GNR 'Atlantics' were put into working order and run on a special train from London to Doncaster on September 20 1953, and back again on the following Sunday. The smaller 'Atlantic' No. 3990 *Henry Oakley* was still in reasonable condition when withdrawn from service in 1937; but when it finished its career some ten years later, the large 'Atlantic' No. 2800 had its superheater removed when it was decided to restore it to its original external appearance as GNR No. 251. My photograph shows the up 'Plant Centenarian' leaving Grantham.

Peter J. Robinson

My 'Glorious Years' in Britain were from 1948, when I first started taking a serious interest in railways, to mid-1967, when those last worthy engines of the great steam designs, the Bulleid 'Pacifics', succumbed to electrification.

I was born in Hexham in 1940, a station which even today remains a steam age time warp with its ex-NER gantry East signalbox, semaphore signalling, some *still* with paraffin lamps, and its Victorian ironmongery. It was in the summer of 1948 that a flash flood severed the East Coast Main Line between Berwick and Dunbar, by washing away several bridges. Services were maintained by diverting to and from Carlisle over the Waverley route and thence by the most northerly trans-Pennine link to Newcastle on which Hexham lies – 40 miles from Carlisle and 20 miles from Newcastle. I spent every waking hour at the station, marvelling at the non-stop passage of all the main Anglo-Scottish services behind the usual ex-LNER 'Pacifics' and 'V2s'. Much freight was also diverted bringing classes rarely seen such as 'WDs' and 'B16s'.

After the main line reopened there was still more than enough to absorb my interest at Hexham. The small engine shed provided power for the local commuter services to Newcastle, for which it had an allocation of five 'G5' 0-4-4Ts, at that time over 50 years old, but still entirely masters of their daily duties. Hexham shed also worked the daily goods over the long rambling ex-NBR branch to Riccarton Junction on the Waverley route, for which it had a 'J36' 0-6-0 No. 65295. This locomotive also worked an evening pick-up freight to Addison Yard, just west of Blaydon. I remember overhearing a discussion in the enginemen's mess-room about the odd occasion when this freight had a load of over 100 wagons for the last (level) short stretch from Clara Vale colliery near Ryton. In today's TOPS-regulated days an unbraked load of such magnitude with a locomotive of less power than a Class '20' diesel is almost incredible.

My memories of these halcyon days are warmed by the kindness of so many railwaymen:

• The shed foreman at St Margaret's engine sheds in Edinburgh, who, when requested by my father on a family two-week holiday in that city in the summer

The last 'stamping ground' for the ex-LNER 'Pacifics' was the ex-LMS service between Glasgow and Aberdeen. Perth was the ideal centre for tackling these trains which were principally the preserve of 'A4s', but in 1963, when this picture was taken, there were still one or two 'A2s' in traffic. This is No. 60527 *Sun Chariot* passing Luncarty working the 6.50pm class 'H' freight from Perth Yard to Craiginches. It had failed earlier in the day, having been removed from the 1.30pm Aberdeen-Glasgow at Perth due to steaming badly as a result of a collapsed brick arch, and was being returned to its home depot of Ferryhill on this freight for repair. This enabled me to speak to the Aberdeen crew at Perth, Friarton Shed and request some exhaust and they duly obliged. How I miss the affinity which I developed with such footplate crews, many of whom sent charming letters of thanks for the print I invariably sent later.

of 1950, happily devoted a member of staff for a whole morning to conducting a delighted and increasingly dirty 10-year-old boy around every corner of what must be a strong contender for Britain's messiest depot. I obtained my very first published photographs of a 'Y9' and, surprisingly, Fowler dock tank No. 47162, on that visit. The 2/6d reproduction fee seemed almost a fortune!

• Many of the Hexham drivers invited me onto the footplate of their 'G5s' whilst they were running round and stabling their stock after arrival with their five-coach commuter trains from Newcastle.

• Numerous Blaydon drivers, particularly Arthur Nicholson and Jack Stonebanks, who were kind enough to allow me to accompany them on the footplate between Hexham and Reedsmouth on the 4.30pm Newcastle to Hawick. At Reedsmouth we changed over with a Hawick crew and returned to Hexham with their mount. Blaydon shed had two 'D49' 4-4-0s for this duty, No. 62747 *The Percy* (appropriately) and No. 62771 *The Rufford*. Hawick used one of their 'D30s' among which were No. 62423 *Dugald Dalgetty*, No. 62428 *The Talisman*, No. 62435 *Norna*, No. 62440 *Wandering Willie* and No. 62430 *Jingling Geordie*. What fabulous, evocative names, which mean so much more to me than simply characters in the Walter Scott novels.

• Several of the Carlisle (Canal) drivers who worked about 50 per cent of the Newcastle-Carlisle trains were equally welcoming and I often rode with them on my Saturday outings to Newcastle or Carlisle. The motive power variety on such trains was considerable. Although Carlisle had five 'B1' 4-6-0s in the early 1950s, two of their turns were frequently worked by a Scottish engine

I had been viewing the impending closure in June 1965 of the remote and scenic line from Dumfries to Stranraer with great regret as I had achieved so few pictures on a line with such potential. But to my delight I discovered from the North Eastern Region Special Traffic Notice that three troop trains from Stranraer to West Woodburn were due to run on Sunday May 16 1965. They were booked for Class '6' power and, on the day, two 'Clans' and one 'Jubilee' provided the power between Stranraer and Newcastle. Of course they had to return, and as the weather was poor on May 16 I hoped for better weather on May 30. In fact, Kingsmoor managed three 'Clans' *and* they were booked to be assisted between Dumfries and Lochanhead – a stiff climb of about five miles, including three miles at 1-in-75. This is the second train with Nos. 45432 and 72007 *Clan MacIntosh* hard at work keeping their ten ex-LMS corridors on the move towards the end of the climb.

filling in between Waverley route turns, and anything could turn up. I remember returning from Carlisle one Sunday evening on the 7pm to Newcastle on the footplate of Eastfield 'V4' No. 61701 (unofficially *Bantam Hen*).

These are but a tiny few of the innumerable kindnesses I have been shown by so many railwaymen and it is, therefore, no surprise that I still have an interest in railways which borders on addiction.

As I grew older I wanted to record as much of this 'magic' as possible and I turned to photography to achieve this. Unfortunately, my means were very limited and my first Brownie box camera had a vicious hair spring shutter speeded at an inconsistent 1/30 second. I was therefore restricted to still shots of locomotives, and even so, for more important shots, my younger brother was deputed to watch the camera carefully, and if he adjudged it to have moved, I took another!

By the age of 16 (1956) I managed to purchase an ADOX Golf folding 2¼in x 3¼in camera with a 1/250 second top speed which removed the risk of camera shake, but I continued to take mainly stills in depots. Those were the days of the RCTS marathon shed-bash bus tours, presided over by our 'Mr RCTS' in the north-east, the dearly loved and now sadly missed Ken Cockerill. Itineraries were ambitious and often chaotic. We usually went by train to the chosen area, then used a local bus company to tour the sheds. Memories flood back:
• Marvelling at sparkling ex-GWR '56XX' 0-6-2Ts on a 2am visit to Ferndale in the Rhondda Fawr Valley.
• Holding a wet hanky over our noses when visiting Mexborough on a Sunday

Taken on one of the day trips to the Grantham area mentioned in the text, the doyen of the 'A4s' No. 60014 *Silver Link* makes a vigorous start southbound from Grantham with an up Newcastle express in the summer of 1960. The louring sky suggests an impending downpour but it has certainly helped the pure white exhaust to stand out well. Although No. 60014 was working through, many trains used to change engines at Grantham and at the time of this picture the shed there maintained a stud of beautifully kept 'A3s'. Sadly *Silver Link* had only two of its 27 years left when this picture was taken – no wonder we initially reviled the 'Deltics' when they supplanted the 'A4s'. I eventually came to admire them but not in the same way I loved the 'Pacifics'.

Just as the freezing fog started to thin and lift on this November Saturday morning in 1964. the 11am Carlisle-Glasgow St Enoch via Dumfries stopping train hauled by 'Clan' class 4-6-2 No. 72008 *Clan MacLeod*, already running a fortuitous 30 minutes late, came to a stand at the signal at the south end of Etterby Bridge, Carlisle. It stood for ten minutes while the sun miraculously penetrated the gloom, and then, when he got the road, the driver immediately set out to make up the lost time. The dramatic scene has been immeasurably improved by the cylinder drain cock stuck open on the other side, the resultant blanket of steam almost affording a silhouette of loco and train. Thank goodness it was the other side! Note the ex-LNER Thompson non-corridor coach at the rear of the short train and 'one man and his dog' watching the action from the river bank at the left.

evening when huge numbers of '04' and 'WD' 2-8-0s were being lit up and the single-ended shed was filled with acrid sulphur-laden smoke.

• Struggling round Colwick, where several of the 'J50' and 'J52' 0-6-0Ts were so dirty that they could only be identified by feeling the works or smoke box number plates.

• Arriving at Stafford Road Works in Wolverhampton hours later than the time on our permit, necessitating the handing over of several bottles of Newcastle Brown Ale to persuade the watchman to let us go round unconducted. No H&S regulations then!

Although my interest was not really in seeing as many engines as possible, I remain grateful that these trips enabled me to see virtually all of this country – much of it off the beaten track.

In 1958 I started work in a Newcastle bank and bought a car, a 1936 MG SA 2-litre drophead coupé, which did about 15mpg. I could only afford to run it if three or four friends shared the cost of the petrol, but it did enable me to enjoy several superb holidays covering Scotland, the south of England – Kent to Cornwall – and Wales.

The most memorable trips were the day trips to Grantham. This involved a 5am start from Hexham, and after picking up a car load at Newcastle we could reach Grantham by about noon after fighting our way through Darlington, Boroughbridge, Doncaster, Retford and Newark – virtually no dual carriageways or by-passes then.

More memories:

• No. 60800 *Green Arrow*, in typical Top Shed condition, flat out, working the up 'Scarborough Flyer' with 13 on, thrashing into Stoke Tunnel at about 50mph and leaving a string of small lineside fires from sparks emitted from the chimney.

• The passage, at about 90mph, of a '9F' 2-10-0 on the down 'Heart of Midlothian', made all the more memorable as I was caught unawares and it passed within about three feet, the rods a complete blur and my feet tingling from the centrifugal force, the whirling motion transmitted through the track. I had a lineside permit but our day revolved round southbound trains climbing Stoke Bank; down trains we just let go – no exhaust! After a curry at the Golden Phoenix Chinese Restaurant in Doncaster we would get home about 2am on the following Sunday – ample time to get a rest before attacking the 10.35am and 11am Sunday Newcastle departures for Kings Cross – both booked for Top Shed 'A4s' and 'caught', whenever the sun was out, leaving Newcastle or Durham.

The last regular steam-hauled express passenger working on the West Coast Main Line was the Sunday morning Liverpool and Manchester-Glasgow which in 1967 was diagrammed for a Kingmoor 'Britannia' 4-6-2. In earlier years an ex-LMS '7P' was more usual. The 'Britannias' were poor performers, mainly because they would only steam if worked hard and, this was not necessary with the LMS 'Scots' and 'Pacifics'. A Polmadie crew worked this train throughout – a formidable challenge with a run-down steam engine and 13 coaches from Preston – no bankers either on a Sunday by 1967. Timekeeping was poor. Here on a blustery March Sunday in 1967 No. 70049 *Solway Firth* is within one mile of its namesake as it jogs along near Rockcliffe. I decided to pan it, just to do something different, and on this occasion this rather hit-and-miss technique proved successful. *Solway Firth* was the last steam engine to be named, receiving its plates without ceremony in May 1960, only six-and-a-half years before withdrawal on December 9 1967. One of the nameplates, purchased from BR for £15, is displayed in our home.

Sadly, the Super Ikonta to which I had progressed by 1959 was rather inconsistent, suffering from camera shake and film buckle, and in 1962 I went back in time and purchased for £25 a Zeiss Contessa Nettel 9cm x 12cm plate camera with a 1/1000 second focal plane shutter. It had six double dark slides and I used to carry a large light-proof changing bag in case I took more than 12 pictures in a day. It gave a quality of definition unequalled by film and I certainly had eradicated the film buckle problem.

By this time steam was on the way out and pursuit of the remaining steam-hauled services became a 'race against time'. The MG had to go – it was replaced by a more conventional mass-produced tin can but I still hanker after it over 30 years later. Distance was no object in the pursuit of steam.

The Worcester 'Castles' on the Cotswold line were a big attraction. My plate camera caused rather an incident in our Worcester hotel. I preferred to change my plates in a wardrobe if the room was dark enough and, on this occasion, after climbing in – there were two drawers at the bottom – to my horror the whole thing fell forward with a terrible crash trapping me inside. Fortunately, I was sharing a room with my lifelong friend Alan Thompson who, when he recovered from the shock, got out of bed and manfully raised the wardrobe to enable me to climb out. No one in the hotel mentioned it and I often wonder how long I might have been trapped if I had been alone.

Then there were the 'Duchesses'. Having done justice to the LNER 'Pacifics' in the late 1950s, I regretted that I had seen so little of the ex-LMS power, and as 'Princess Royals', 'Duchesses', 'Scots', 'Patriots' and 'Jubilees' were still

The last time I saw a 'Patriot' in action. Despite being in her last few months of working life No. 45550 is going well past Shap Quarry, working a 13-coach empty stock train from Carlisle to Morecambe in August 1962. I am indebted to my friend Stephen Crook for cleaning the engine – he hadn't time to tackle the tender! – and note the dome! Although obviously in fine fettle, this was one of her last runs – with the other surviving member of the class, No. 45543, she was placed into store at Preston shortly afterwards and withdrawn in November 1962.

In the last week of their lives four of the last 'J27s' huddle companionably together inside the Sunderland roundhouse in September 1967. I can almost feel their apprehension at their uncertain fate. With a combined age of 208 years they will have repaid their initial cost hundreds of times and must rank as one of the most successful British locomotives. Nos. 65811 and 65855 were both 59, whereas Nos. 65879 and 65882 were both mere youngsters of 45! The latter two were built with superheated boilers, but both received saturated boilers towards the end of the Second World War.

Opposite Steam engines seem to me to be imbued with human characteristics, and 'J27' No. 65882 appears to be blinking at the bright sunlight as it emerges from the gloom of the ex-NER roundhouse at Sunderland, to undertake two trips up the Silksworth branch on a September afternoon in 1967. Looking at least seven months pregnant, these doughty 0-6-0s were introduced in 1904. No. 65882, however, was new in August 1922, and was thus 45 years old by this time, having spent its whole life on heavy mineral trains in the north-east. Together with their 'Q6' relatives, the 'J27s' were the last steam engines to work in the north-east – by the end of September 1967 they were cold for ever. I am proud to be a founder member of the North Eastern Locomotive Preservation Group, which was formed in 1967 to preserve a 'J27'. As a result, No. 65894, the last built, was purchased and restored to working order. I have been treasurer of this Group for 20 years now and derive great pleasure from seeing this typical ex-NER 'collier' in action on the North Yorkshire Moors Railway.

in action around Carlisle I spent every possible minute on the lines radiating from that city.

On Sundays the up 'Royal Scot' stopped at Penrith and by judicious use of minor roads it was possible to get a shot on the 'cold' climb out of Carlisle and another south of Penrith. This involved speeds of up to 100mph in my MG 1300 GT and I have a vivid memory of rounding a bend near Calthwaite to be confronted by an oncoming vicar driving in the middle of the road. I couldn't possibly stop but horn and headlight alerted the worthy cleric – my last glimpse of him was the rear of his A40 disappearing through a hedge into a field. He would have been no bother if he had been on his own side of the road, but I am thankful he wasn't a herd of cows!

My last sight of an '8P' on the 'Sunday Scot' was on December 31 1963 when No. 46250 *City of Lichfield* – one of the more attractive joined-up-front-footplating class members – took over at Carlisle from a failed diesel. It was a crisp frosty day and the sight and sound of that magnificent machine fully master of its task is a memory I shall cherish always. Thankfully both shots – at Wreay and Clifton – were OK and can still evoke a misty eye.

In April 1966 I was obliged to move to London and while I reviled both the lifestyle and work in the City, it did make it easier to cover the last days of steam in the Isle of Wight and on the LSWR main line to Bournemouth and Weymouth. After the Bulleids succumbed in July and the ex-NER steam engines finished in the north-east in September 1967, there were only a few steam survivors in the north-west, but I found them of little interest when compared with a few years earlier.

I turned to the Continent for solace and found some really superb steam designs behind the Iron Curtain, with the Czech 4-8-2s and the Romanian 2-8-4s particularly impressive. Unfortunately, the oppressive regimes resulted in one or two brief spells of imprisonment – the longest six hours – but thanks to my just-about-adequate German I always managed to talk my way out of it – the secret police were very bemused by the antique camera and plates but never confiscated nor developed any. I wasn't married then and felt that the magnificence of the locomotives justified the enervation – as long as you kept on the move it was OK. I certainly gain great pleasure from the pictures I obtained – forbidden fruit always tastes sweeter!

'Glorious Years' indeed!

The Glorious Years

The 'Glorious Years' series is one of the longest-running features in *Steam Railway* magazine. On this page is listed for the first time all the contributors to date. Originally mostly black and white work was included – later when the magazine became full colour, some authors made a second contribution of colour pictures.

Which years actually constitute the 'Glorious Years' is a very personal and subjective matter, so any period until 1968 is covered. The magazine is always looking for new contributions – if you have a selection of images from your 'Glorious Years', either black and white or colour, please submit them to the editor at *Steam Railway* magazine, EMAP Apex Publications, Apex House, Oundle Road, Peterborough PE2 9NP, telephone 01733 898100.

Steam Railway, published on the first Friday each month and available from all good newsagents, is the world's biggest-selling steam magazine. Its unique blend of the best of steam action from the past with the current scene makes it an unmissable read. Each issue is packed with news, views and features, all presented with stunning pictures from Britain's leading railway photographers.

Issue No./Cover Date/Photographer

1 April 1981 W. J. V. Anderson
2 May 1981 Brian Morrison
3 June 1981 Mike Esau
4 July 1981 Les Nixon
5 August 1981 Geoff Rixon
6 September 1981 R. C. Riley
7 October 1981 Ian Krause
8 November 1981 C. R. L. Coles
9 December 1981 Stanley Creer
10 January 1982 Gavin Morrison
11 February 1982 Ivo Peters
12 March 1982 Maurice Earley
13 April 1982 Colin T. Gifford
14 May 1982 Philip Lynch
15 June 1982 John Vaughan
16 July 1982 Henry Casserley
17 August 1982 John Whiteley
18 September 1982 Dr. Gerald Siviour
19 October 1982 John Goss
20 November 1982 John Cooper-Smith
21 December 1982 Eric Sawford
22 January 1983 Derek Cross
23 February 1983 Robert Leslie
24 March 1983 Roger Siviter ARPS
25 April 1983 Tony Richardson
26 May 1983 John Paige
27 June 1983 George Heiron
28 July 1983 John Hillier
29 August 1983 David Idle
30 September 1983 Ian R. Smith
31 October 1983 Malcolm Dunnett
32 November 1983 Tom Boustead
49 May 1984 Geoffrey Jefferson
50 June 1984 Eric Oldham
51 July 1984 Jim Carter
52 August 1984 David Hepburne-Scott
53 September 1984 Arthur Haynes
54 October 1984 C. C. B. Herbert
55 November 1984 Eric Bruton
56 December 1984 Peter J. Robinson
57 January 1985 Geoff Silcock
58 February 1985 Richard Evans
59 March 1985 Cliff Sarah
60 April 1985 Nigel Dychoff
61 May 1985 Tony Butcher
62 June 1985 Colin Boocock
63 July 1985 Peter Hughes
64 August 1985 John Scrace
65 September 1985 John Ashman
66 October 1985 R. J. Blenkinsop
67 November 1985 Neville Stead
68 December 1985 Alan Bailey
69 January 1986 John Snell
70 February 1986 Vic Allen
71 March 1986 Tom Heavyside
72 April 1986 Chris Gammell
73 May 1986 Ernest Glen
74 June 1986 Mike Fox
75 July 1986 David Sellman
76 August 1986 Maurice Burns
77 September 1986 Duncan Gomershall
78 October 1986 Harold James

79 November 1986 John Henton
80 December 1986 Peter Cookson
81 January 1987 Douglas Doherty
82 February 1987 Brian Rutherford
83 March 1987 Edwin Wilmshurst
84 April 1987 Alan Corkhill
85 May 1987 Peter Barnfield
86 June 1987 Tony Ross
87 July 1987 Bob Clarke
88 August 1987 Michael Mensing
89 September 1987 Alan Whitehead
90 October 1987 John Gilks
91 November 1987 Frank Hornby
92 December 1987 Alan Bowler
93 January 1988 Paul Cooper
94 February 1988 David Canning
95 March 1988 David Percival
96 April 1988 Peter Hay
97 May 1988 David Anderson
98 June 1988 John Everitt
99 July 1988 Tony Brown
100 August 1988 John Hunt
101 September 1988 Philip Wells
102 October 1988 Tim Mills
103 November 1988 Norman Preedy
104 December 1988 Robin Russell
105 January 1989 Mike Morant
106 February 1989 Kenneth Oldham
107 March 1989 John Nunn
108 April 1989 Derek Buckett
109 May 1989 Peter Winding
110 June 1989 John Dagley-Morris
111 July 1989 Paul Strong (part 1)
112 August 1989 Paul Strong (part 2)
113 September 1989 Wilf Underhay
114 October 1989 Nigel Kendal
115 November 1989 Trevor Ermel
116 December 1989 Kenneth Leech
117 January 1990 Tony Porter
118 February 1990 Barrie Walker
119 March 1990 Derrick Dant
120 April 1990 Ken Groundwater
121 May 1990 Reg Batten
122 June 1990 Jim Winkley (part 1)
123 July 1990 Jim Winkley (part 2)
124 August 1990 Bryan Hicks
125 September 1990 Dugald Cameron
126 October 1990 David Gouldthorp
127 November 1990 Wyn Hobson
128 December 1990 O. S. Nock
129 January 1991 David Eatwell
130 February 1991 Frank Dean
131 March 1991 Hugh Ballantyne
132 April 1991 A. E. 'Dusty' Durrant
133 May 1991 Dr. Ian C. Allen
134 June 1991 Dick Jelves
135 July 1991 Margaret Radway
136 August 1991 Terry Nicholls
137 September 1991 Patrick Kingston
138 October 1991 Peter Coton
139 November 1991 Dennis Tebbutt
140 December 1991 Ralph Ward

141 January 1992 Derek Huntriss
142 February 1992 Dave Marriott
143 March 1992 Ken Fairey
144 April 1992 Les Reason
145 May 1992 David Hughes
146 June 1992 Paul Riley (part 1)
147 July 1992 Paul Riley (part 2)
148 August 1992 Noel Machell (part 1)
149 September 1992 Noel Machell (part 2)
150 October 1992   R. J. Blenkinsop, Mike Esau, Gavin Morrison, R. C. Riley, Geoff Rixon, John Whiteley
151 November 1992 Mike Esau
152 December 1992 R. J. Blenkinsop
153 January 1993 Les Nixon (part 1)
154 February 1993 Les Nixon (part 2)
155 March 1993 Keith Pirt (part 1)
156 April 1993 Keith Pirt (part 2)
157 May 1993 Ron Robinson (part 1)
158 June 1993 Ron Robinson (part 2)
159 July 1993 Terry Flinders (part 1)
160 August 1993 Terry Flinders (part 2)
161 September 1993 Graham Bell (part 1)
162 October 1993 Graham Bell (part 2)
163 November 1993 Don Rutter
164 December 1993 Allan Heyes
165 January 1994 Ben Ashworth (part 1)
166 February 1994 Ben Ashworth (part 2)
167 March 1994 Andy Elliott (part 1)
168 April 1994 Andy Elliott (part 2)
169 May 1994 Gerry Drought (part 1)
170 June 1994 Gerry Drought (part 2)
171 July 1994 Leslie Sandler
172 August 1994 Maurice Edwards (part 1)
173 September 1994 Maurice Edwards (part 2)
174 October 1994 Eric Woods (part 1)
175 November 1994 Eric Woods (part 2)
176 December 1994 Neville Knight
177 January 1995 John Clarke (part 1)
178 February 1995 John Clarke (part 2)
179 March 1995 G. P. Keen
180 April 1995 Peter Rose
181 May 1995 Graham Morgan
182 June 1995 Chris Nettleton
183 July 1995 Norman Glover (part 1)
184 August 1995 Norman Glover (part 2)
185 September 1995 Klaus Marx
186 October 1995 John Barrance (part 1)
187 November 1995 John Barrance (part 2)
188 December 1995 Dave Thomas
189 January 1996 Colin Hogg (part 1)
190 February 1996 Colin Hogg (part 2)
191 March 1996 Paul Beko (part 1)
192 April 1996 Paul Beko (part 2)
193 May 1996 Paul Leavens (part 1)
194 June 1996 Paul Leavens (part 2)
195 July 1996 Neil Sprinks

Note: 'The Glorious Years' April 1981 to November 1983 appeared in *Steam World* magazine.